M Yourselves Saviours of Men

Dag Heward-Mills

Parchment House

MAKE YOURSELVES SAVIOURS OF MEN

First published 2019 by Parchment House
1st Printing 2019

Find out more about Dag Heward-Mills at:

Healing Jesus Campaign
Email: evangelist@daghewardmills.org
Website: www.daghewardmills.org
Facebook: Dag Heward-Mills
Twitter: @EvangelistDag

ISBN: 978-1-64329-210-6

Contents

Chapter 1

Make Yourselves Saviours of Men

And SAVIOURS SHALL COME UP on mount Zion to judge the mount of Esau; and the kingdom shall be the Lord's.

Obadiah 1:21

Obadiah gives a great prophecy of the coming of saviours. Who are these saviours? I thought Jesus Christ was the Saviour? Indeed, Jesus Christ is the Saviour of the world! We all love the scripture that tells us that a saviour was born to us in the city of David.

For unto you is born this day in the city of David A SAVIOUR, which is Christ the Lord.

Luke 2:11

Even though Jesus is the Saviour of the world, there is something we are supposed to do to save people. In a sense, that makes us also saviours of men. What are we supposed to do to save men? We are supposed to preach the gospel and share the love of Jesus everywhere.

Jesus Christ died on the cross two thousand years ago but many people do not know what happened on the cross. Jesus Christ exerted great effort and paid a high price so that men could be saved. It is interesting though, that people cannot be saved without us preaching about Jesus. How can they know about Jesus if they have not ever been told? How can they hear if no one has ever been sent to them?

How then shall they call on him in whom they have not believed? And how shall they believe in him of whom they have not heard? and how shall they hear without a preacher? And how shall they preach, except they be sent? as it is written, How beautiful are the feet of them that preach the gospel of peace, and bring glad tidings of good things!

Romans 10:14-15

People who live today are not aware of events that have taken place in the past. It is normal for events, no matter how dramatic they were, to be forgotten quite soon after they occurred. Indeed, this is the reason why history is studied in school. People do not just happen to know what happened in the past.

Events fade away and often repeat themselves in naturally recurring cycles. The death of Jesus Christ was an unfortunate event where an innocent man was lumped together with criminals and executed unjustly. Unjust executions have been occurring for centuries. The wickedness, the betrayal, the cruelty and the religious madness that was exhibited at the cross were nothing so unusual in the history of mankind. It should have been forgotten within a few months of the event. Jesus knew that His death on the cross was nothing unusual in the lives of wicked men. It was nothing to write home about. Wicked men are always wicked!

It was important that the rest of the world would know of the story of Jesus Christ. Why is that? Because as many as believe that Jesus is the Son of God shall be saved!

Indeed, a famous Jewish historian called Josephus wrote a reliable account about what happened in the time of Jesus Christ. Josephus was born in Jerusalem only four years after Jesus was crucified on the cross. His account of Jesus Christ would obviously only be read by history students who study Jewish history. Indeed, there are very few of such history students in the world. Did Jesus Christ die just for history students? Certainly not!

Ordinary people who do not study history also have to know about Jesus Christ and what He has done for us. *If there was no preaching, just a few history students would hear about Jesus Christ.*

The power of God is available for the people that hear and believe the gospel. Salvation comes by faith and faith comes by hearing. If the world is to benefit from this great event of Jesus Christ dying on the cross and shedding His blood as the Lamb of God, people will have to hear about it. We have a duty to tell the whole world about Jesus Christ.

Importance of Last Words

It is no surprise that Jesus' very last words contain a clear commission to go into the whole world to inform people about Jesus Christ. In various different accounts, Christians are asked to go out into the whole world and preach repentance and forgiveness of sins through Jesus Christ.

This last command of Jesus Christ is the basis of this book. Some people call it "The Great Commission". Perhaps, it is called the Great Commission because it is the last and final command of Jesus Christ to His disciples. Final words are special and great words! Last words carry a sense of being the most important words ever spoken by a human being. Since last words are the very last things a person will say, they are likely to be the most important and the most critical things he will ever say.

Last Words are Ominous Words

One of our pastors lay dying in the hospital. He was deathly ill and he knew that he had but a few more days to go. He called his son and asked his son to record his last words. When he died, his family came for his body and took it to a mortuary somewhere in town. They made their plans to bury him in their private family mausoleum. Then his son came up to the family, (comprising mainly of his uncles and aunties) and informed them that he had recorded the very last words of his father.

When the family listened to the last words of his father, they changed their minds about almost everything they were doing. Why was that?

The last words of this pastor were very simple. He said, "When I die, my body should be handed over to Bishop Dag Heward-Mills. Whatever he and the other bishops decide about my funeral should be accepted as final. The bishops should decide where and how I should be buried."

Now, the family, who were sticklers for their traditions about funerals, promptly relinquished his body to the church and asked that I decide everything about the funeral. They were remarkably respectful and submissive to the last words of the dying man.

You see, last words are frightening words. People are afraid of the last words of a person. Perhaps, they feel that "last words" carry some kind of mystical power. They fear that some mischief will befall anyone who goes against the last words of a person.

Danger for Ignoring the "Last Words"

Indeed, a great mischief has befallen the church for ignoring the last words of Jesus Christ. Because we have ignored His instruction to go into the world, the plagues of sin, poverty, debt, homosexuality, fornication and other perversions have fallen on the church. Today, the church is a phantom of what it is supposed to be.

Large parts of the church are powerless and helpless against demon power. The church is a large mass of tiny little spiritual children running around in circles, playing church games. Because the church has ignored the last words of Jesus, it has become an ineffective and powerless group.

Last Words are Important Words

Last words are not only ominous words but also important words. If you had an opportunity to say your very last words to a friend, would you talk about the soap that he should bath with or how he should iron his clothes? Would you not tell him something more important than that?

Would you not say something really deep, meaningful and powerful? Would you not say something that he should remember for the rest of his life? Would you spend your time talking about different types of soap that he could bath with? Let's be serious!

I remember watching a documentary about a flight that was about to crash. There was something wrong with the tail of this jumbo jet and it kept going up and down in a crazy manner until it eventually crashed into a mountainside after an hour of mad flying. There were only one or two survivors. Some of you may know about this crash. Because the plane kept going up and down for an hour, everyone on board knew they were doomed. It was only a matter of time before they crashed.

When the search and rescue party arrived on the scene, they found many dead people. Amazingly, many of the passengers had written final and farewell letters to their loved ones. During the time that the plane was zigzagging across the sky, many had written their last words for their loved ones. Some of these letters were found in the pockets and bags of the dead passengers. What a sad story!

I always wondered what these doomed passengers wrote to their loved ones. Don't you think they wrote about something important? Do you think they wrote about the food to give to their dog? Do you think they wrote about the vet's appointment they had to take their cat to? I don't think so! They must have written something very important because they were writing last words.

When Jesus stood on the Mount of Olives speaking His last words, I don't think He cracked jokes about Peter's love for fish bones, fish eyes and fish skin. I do not think He commented on how He would miss Peter's amazing grilled fish. I do not think He told Peter how He would miss the tilapia in Galilee. Indeed, Jesus spoke about the most important thing of all.

Those last words of Jesus are what are called the Great Commission. The Great Commission could also be called the Last Commission. Hudson Taylor, missionary to China, made the term "Great Commission" popular. I agree with him that it is the Great Commission. It certainly was the last commission of Jesus. It stands out from everything else Jesus said because it was the last commission.

Amazingly, you will find that the last words in many of the New Testament books contain a variation of this last and great commission. This last and great commission is important because it makes it clear that Christians have an obligation towards the sinners in our world. Indeed, we have an obligation to make ourselves saviours of men.

It was William Carey (missionary to India) who wrote a book entitled *"An Enquiry into the Obligations of Christians to Use Means for the Conversion of the Heathen."* It was William Booth (founder of The Salvation Army) who encouraged us "to make ourselves saviours of men."

These great men only echoed the words of Jesus Christ. They have only repeated the great commission in their own words. "Make yourselves saviours of men!" Indeed, we must make ourselves saviours of men! By repeating the stories of Jesus Christ and telling people how great He is and how He saved us on the cross, we make ourselves saviours of men.

We are under a great obligation towards the sinners and the heathen of this world. We are under an obligation to speak! We are under obligation to go! We are under obligation to preach! We are under obligation to pray! We are under obligation to fight for the souls of men! We are under obligation to make ourselves saviours of men! We have no other choice than to preach the gospel of Jesus Christ. It is time to listen carefully to the last and great words of our Saviour, Jesus Christ.

Chapter 2

Where Was the Great Commission Delivered?

GO YE THEREFORE, AND TEACH ALL NATIONS, BAPTIZING THEM IN THE NAME OF THE FATHER, AND OF THE SON, AND OF THE HOLY GHOST: Teaching them to observe all things whatsoever I have commanded you: and, lo, I am with you alway, even unto the end of the world. Amen.

Matthew 28:19-20

I t is obvious that the Great Commission was repeated in various forms and in different places. At various times and at various places Jesus' last words seemed to be similar. Slight variations of the Great Commission seemed to be given at different places and at different times. Beware of repeated last words!

1. Matthew's Great Commission was given on a mountain in Galilee.

Then THE ELEVEN DISCIPLES WENT AWAY INTO GALILEE, INTO A MOUNTAIN where Jesus had appointed them...

And Jesus came and spake unto them, saying, all power is given unto me in heaven and in earth. GO YE THEREFORE, AND TEACH ALL NATIONS, baptizing them in the name of the Father, and of the Son, and of the Holy Ghost: Teaching them to observe all things whatsoever I have commanded you: and, lo, I am with you alway, even unto the end of the world. Amen.

Matthew 28:16, 18-20

2. Mark's Great Commission was given when He appeared to His disciples at dinnertime.

AFTERWARD HE APPEARED UNTO THE ELEVEN AS THEY SAT AT MEAT, and upbraided them with their unbelief and hardness of heart, because they believed not them which had seen him after he was raised.

And he said unto them, GO YE INTO ALL THE WORLD, AND PREACH THE GOSPEL TO EVERY CREATURE. He that believeth and is baptized shall be saved; but he that believeth not shall be damned.

And these signs shall follow them that believe; In my name shall they cast out devils; they shall speak with new tongues; They shall take up serpents; and if they drink any deadly thing, it shall not hurt them; they shall lay hands on the sick, and they shall recover.

Mark 16:14-18

3. Luke's Great Commission was given at a dinner in Jerusalem.

And they rose up the same hour, and RETURNED TO JERUSALEM, AND FOUND THE ELEVEN GATHERED TOGETHER, and them that were with them, Saying, The Lord is risen indeed, and hath appeared to Simon. And they told what things were done in the way, and how he was known of them in breaking of bread.

And as they thus spake, Jesus himself stood in the midst of them, and saith unto them, Peace be unto you. But they were terrified and affrighted, and supposed that they had seen a spirit. And he said unto them, Why are ye troubled? and why do thoughts arise in your hearts? Behold my hands and my feet, that it is I myself: handle me, and see; for a spirit hath not flesh and bones, as ye see me have. And when he had thus spoken, he shewed them his hands and his feet.

And while they yet believed not for joy, and wondered, he said unto them, Have ye here any meat? AND THEY GAVE HIM A PIECE OF A BROILED FISH, and of an honeycomb. And he took it, and did eat before them. And he said unto them, These are the words which I spake unto you, while I was yet with you, that all things must be fulfilled, which were written in the law of Moses, and in the prophets, and in the psalms, concerning me. Then opened he their understanding, that they might understand the scriptures, And said unto them, Thus it is written, and thus it behoved Christ to suffer, and to rise from the dead the third day: AND THAT REPENTANCE AND REMISSION OF SINS SHOULD BE PREACHED IN HIS NAME AMONG ALL NATIONS, BEGINNING AT JERUSALEM.

Luke 24:33-47

4.   John's Great Commission was given by the sea of Tiberias.

AFTER THESE THINGS JESUS SHEWED HIMSELF AGAIN TO THE DISCIPLES AT THE SEA OF TIBERIAS; and on this wise shewed he himself....So when they had dined, Jesus saith to Simon Peter, Simon, son of Jonas, lovest thou me more than these? He saith unto him, Yea, Lord; thou knowest that I love thee. He saith unto him, FEED MY LAMBS.

John 21:1, 15

5.   The Great Commission in Acts was given on the Mount of Olives just before He ascended in a cloud.

But ye shall receive power, after that the Holy Ghost is come upon you: AND YE SHALL BE WITNESSES UNTO ME BOTH IN JERUSALEM, AND IN ALL JUDAEA, AND IN SAMARIA, AND UNTO THE UTTERMOST PART OF THE EARTH. And when he had spoken these things, while they beheld, he was taken up; and a cloud received him out of their sight. And while they looked steadfastly toward heaven as he went up, behold, two men stood by them in white apparel; Which also said, Ye men of Galilee, why stand ye gazing up into heaven? this same Jesus, which is taken up from you into heaven, shall so come in like manner as ye have seen him go into heaven. THEN RETURNED THEY UNTO JERUSALEM FROM THE MOUNT CALLED OLIVET, WHICH IS FROM JERUSALEM A SABBATH DAY'S JOURNEY.

Acts 1:8-12

Chapter 3

Men Have Become Saviours of Themselves

But realize this that in the last days difficult times will come. For men will be LOVERS OF SELF, LOVERS OF MONEY, boastful, arrogant, revilers, disobedient to parents, ungrateful, unholy, unloving, irreconcilable, malicious gossips, without self-control, brutal, haters of good, treacherous, reckless, conceited, LOVERS OF PLEASURE RATHER THAN LOVERS OF GOD, holding to a form of godliness, although they have denied its power; Avoid such men as these.

2 Timothy 3:1-5 (NASB)

I n the last days, men shall be lovers of themselves, lovers of money and lovers of pleasure. These are terrible depravities to which men will fall in the last days. The love for ourselves and the love for money have made us the lowest types of Christians that have ever lived on the face of this earth. We have more knowledge, more resources, more money and more grace than any other generation. Yet we are the ones who are doing the least for the kingdom of God. We are truly the Laodicean, lukewarm church.

After salvation, most Christians assume that Christianity spreads by osmosis. From the pastors to the lowest members of the churches, hardly anyone thinks about the souls of men.

Jesus' ominous last words to His church are ignored with a stunning boldness that raises the question of insanity. *Almost everything else is preached about except soul winning. We have nice times, nice churches, nice feelings, nice programs, nice songs, nice worship nights, nice congregations and nice dignified pastors but no one preaches about soul winning.*

The great last words of Jesus Christ have been set aside. Everyone is silent about the Great Commission. Everyone thinks that someone else will do it. Everyone thinks that someone else will go.

Perhaps, a lady who cannot find a husband will go on the mission field. Perhaps, a boy who dropped out of school will go on the mission. In a recent survey, it was discovered that over sixty percent of the modern church did not know what the Great Commission was.

It is sad to see that the Great Commission is not regarded as a great commission any more. In spite of this, I can tell you that God's work will flourish and souls will be saved, no matter who goes or who does not go.

The "love yourself spirit" of the last days has grounded the church of God. There are now few real evangelists, few church planters and even fewer missionaries.

Chapter 4

The Vision of the Dark and Stormy Ocean

IN THE VISIONS OF GOD BROUGHT HE ME INTO THE LAND of Israel, and set me upon a very high mountain, by which was as the frame of a city on the south. . .

And the man said unto me, Son of man, behold with thine eyes, and hear with thine ears, and SET THINE HEART UPON ALL THAT I SHALL SHEW THEE; for to the intent that I might shew them unto thee art thou brought hither: declare all that thou seest to the house of Israel.

Ezekiel 40:2, 4

William Booth had some amazing visions, which are worth reproducing in this book. They give us a clear picture of Christian behaviour towards the Great Commission. I hope you receive them and I hope they will charge you up as much as they have done me. Make yourselves saviours of men!

William Booth, founder of The Salvation Army, once narrated a vision that he had whilst meditating on the state of the dying souls all around him. Visions from God are given so that we set our hearts on all that we see and hear. This is the vision he had:

The Vision

He saw a dark and stormy ocean. There were black clouds hanging heavily over the sea. Every now and then, there were vivid flashes of lightning and thunder. When the winds moaned, the waves rose and foamed and dipped and rose again. Indeed, anyone who has been in the wild ocean before will know that this is a truly dangerous and deadly place to be.

In that ocean, he saw myriads of poor human beings plunging, floating, shouting and shrieking and cursing and struggling and drowning.

As these poor souls cursed and shrieked, they rose and shrieked again and then sank into the water to rise no more.

Suddenly, he saw in the midst of this dark and angry ocean, a mighty rock that rose up like a mountain in the midst of the sea. Around this great rock, was a platform onto which some of the poor struggling, drowning wretches were continually climbing out of the angry ocean.

William Booth says that he was delighted to see the platform, which was being used as a point of salvation for the struggling souls in the sea. As he continued to observe the scene in the ocean, he noticed some amazing things, which reveal a lot about our behaviour today.

1. ***Saviours of men:*** He noticed that a number of those who were already safe on the platform were helping the poor creatures, still in the angry waters, to reach the same place of safety.

2. ***Organisers of salvation:*** He found a number of those who had been rescued, planning and organising ladders, ropes, rafts, boats and any other equipment that they could use to effectively save some of the poor, struggling creatures from the sea.

3. ***Self Sacrifice:*** He also noticed that there were some of the saved people who actually jumped into the water regardless of all consequences, to rescue the perishing. The sight of the people being saved and the sight of those sacrificial saviours delighted William Booth greatly.

4. ***Most had forgotten:*** William Booth also noticed that although all those on the platforms had been rescued from the sea at one time or another, nearly everyone seemed to have forgotten about it. The memory of the dangerous sea no longer troubled them. The fact that people on the platform did not have any agonising care for the poor perishing ones that were drowning before their very eyes was the most difficult scene to behold. Indeed, many of the drowning and struggling creatures in the sea were friends, husbands or wives, mothers, sisters, brothers and even children of those rescued already.

5. ***Many were unconcerned:*** The next amazing thing to behold was the fact that the people on the platform were aware of what was happening in the sea. There were two reasons for this. First of all, they were living on the platform in full view of the struggling, drowning souls in the water.

    Secondly, those on the platform regularly went to hear lectures in which the awful state of the poor drowning creatures was described. In spite of these facts, most of the people on the platform were unconcerned.

6.   ***Trading in full view:*** Another interesting thing about the occupants of the platform was their different occupations, which they carried out, in full view of the perishing. Many of them were absorbed, day and night, in trading. They did their trading to make gain and to store up their savings in boxes and strong rooms.

7.   ***Growing Flowers on the Rock:*** Some of the people on the platform were actually spending their time growing flowers on the side of rock. Others were painting pieces of cloth or playing music. Some were dressing themselves up in different styles and walking about to be admired. Others occupied themselves in eating and drinking. All this was done in full view of the poor struggling creatures that were drowning in the water all around them.

8.   ***Arguments on the Rock:*** Some of the people on the platform were taken up with arguing about the poor drowning creatures. The arguments had to do with what would become of them in the future.

9.   ***Religious Ceremonies on the Rock:*** Whilst beholding the strugglers in the sea, some of the people on the platform contented themselves with holding curious religious ceremonies. By carrying out these ceremonies, they felt content that they had performed their duty towards the perishing creatures.

10.   ***The Higher Platform:*** William Booth now looked more closely and noticed that some of the people who had come onto the rock had discovered a path that led to a higher platform away from the black clouds and stormy ocean. From that higher platform, they expected to be carried away one day to the main land. Those on this higher platform passed their time away with pleasant thoughts, congratulating themselves on their good fortune in being rescued from the stormy oceans. They sang songs about the happiness that they would experience when taken to the main land.

11. ***The Great Being:*** Suddenly, the miseries, agonies, quarrels and blasphemies of these poor struggling people in this dark sea moved the pity of the great God so much that He sent a Great Being to save them. This Great Being leaped right into the raging sea, among the drowning sinking people, where he toiled to rescue them with great cries, tears and sweat and bloodied hands. As the Great Being toiled, he continually cried to those already rescued to help him.

12. ***No Help for the Great Being:*** Another strange thing was that those on the platform heard the Great Being calling for help but did not take heed nor care about him. They said they loved him very much and were in full sympathy with him in the task he had undertaken. In fact, they worshipped him and professed to do so. But they were so taken up with their professions, their money saving, their pleasures, their families and their nice activities.

13. ***Make us more secure:*** Perhaps the strangest of all things was that those on the platform were actually crying to the Great Being to come out of the water and spend some time with them to make them even happier than they were. Some wanted him to come and make them more secure on the rock. Others wanted him to come and take away various doubts and misgivings that they had. They would cry to the Great Being who was in the water with the poor struggling drowning creatures, "Come to us! Come and help us!"

14. ***A Clear Vision:*** This vision is not difficult to interpret. You do not need to be a rocket scientist to understand it. The rock was the place of salvation. All those drowning in the water are the dying shrieking, struggling, agonising multitudes who are going to hell. The Great Being is Jesus Christ who was sent to save people. The people on the rock are the unconcerned Christians who fill our churches today.

15. ***A True Vision:*** How true this vision is! It describes us in great detail. We cannot escape the description of the unconcerned church who have not made themselves saviours of men.

This vision shows us that saved people have neglected their God-given work of saving souls. It is the obligation of the Christian church to save many souls.

Chapter 5

The Great Commission According to Matthew

And when they saw him, they worshipped him: but some doubted. And Jesus came and spake unto them, saying, All power is given unto me in heaven and in earth. GO YE THEREFORE, AND TEACH ALL NATIONS, BAPTIZING THEM IN THE NAME OF THE FATHER, AND OF THE SON, AND OF THE HOLY GHOST: TEACHING THEM To observe all things whatsoever I have commanded you: and, lo, I am with you alway, even unto the end of the world. Amen.

Matthew 28:17-20

Each and every one of the apostles repeated the Great Commission because they were the last words of Jesus Christ to us all. Let us look at this great commission in detail. Perhaps God will speak to you about your God-given role in the Great Commission.

According to Matthew, these were the last words of Jesus Christ. This commission was given on one of the mountains of Galilee. (Matthew 28:16). There are a series of mountains that surround the lake of Galilee. These words that Jesus spoke on one of these mountains are what we call The Great Commission. Let us go through the highlights of this Great Commission according to Matthew. Make yourselves saviours of men!

1.   THE GREAT COMMISSION IS A COMMISSION OF POWER:

Jesus said all power has been given to Him! You must preach the gospel with power, with signs and with wonders. Yet, most Christians have gone into the world without the power of God. Teaching with PowerPoint, computers and projectors is not the same as teaching with miracles, signs and wonders. Many parts of the world need a demonstration of God's power. You must become a minister of God with real power demonstration!

2.   THE GREAT COMMISSION IS A COMMISSION TO GO:

Jesus said, "Go!" Yet most Christians have stayed. Few churches send anybody anywhere. Few pastors send anyone anywhere. It is a commission to move and yet the church is stationary. We stay in our nice churches! We stay in our nice countries. We stay in our comfortable homes. Most of the church is not going anywhere.

3.   THE GREAT COMMISSION IS A COMMISSION TO TEACH:

Jesus said, "Teach!" The Great Commission is a commission to teach. Teach what? It is not a commission to teach economics, business, physics, chemistry or history. Do you think that Jesus Christ is sending you out to teach economics, business or history? You must be joking! He is not doing that. These subjects did not even exist in His day. He is sending us out to teach the word of God.

The commission to teach implies the need to stay in a place longer. This is how churches are formed. Indeed, the Great Commission, according to Matthew is a commission to plant churches so that teaching can come on. It is not possible to teach much in a day. It is not possible to teach much in two days. You have to live with people if you are going to teach them anything. This is where church planting becomes important. We can conclude safely, therefore, that the Great Commission is also a commission to plant churches.

4. THE GREAT COMMISSION IS A COMMISSION TO BAPTIZE:

Jesus said, "Baptize!" Yet many do not baptize anyone in water. We sprinkle water on babies and claim that they are baptized. Baptism must accompany salvation. Every great commissioner must be a baptizer of souls.

5. THE GREAT COMMISSION IS A COMMISSION TO ALL NATIONS:

Jesus said, "Go to all nations!" Most Christians have not gone to many nations. Few churches reach out beyond their communities. If you search the Internet, you will find very few international ministries.

Few churches ever look beyond their horizon to see if there are souls that need their good news. Churches are happy with their nice times, nice games, nice conferences, nice get-togethers, nice Easter and Christmas parties, nice choirs, nice lights and nice families.

We are expected to go to all nations. Because we do not go to nations, some nations are totally overwhelmed with other religions. There is a clear correlation between the religion in a country and the fulfilment of the commission by obedient commissioners. Wherever a great commissioner went, that nation turned to Jesus Christ.

I once visited Malta and found a nation which claimed to be Christian. They claimed to be Christian because Apostle Paul was marooned on that island. His going to that island turned the whole island to Christ. Wherever a great commissioner goes, the nation turns to Christ.

I once visited Chennai in the southern part of India. I was told that this part of India had a lot of Christians. Apparently, doubting Thomas the disciple of Jesus, had gone to Chennai as a great commissioner of the gospel. The rest of India did not have the blessing of having a great commissioner so it fell to other religions.

Failing to obey the Great Commission of Jesus Christ is the reason why many people are not saved today. Entire nations and regions have fallen to darkness because believers would not even talk about the Great Commission of Jesus.

6.   *THE GREAT COMMISSION IS A COMMISSION OF HIS PRESENCE.*

Jesus said, "Lo, I am with you alway, even unto the end of the world." In the Great Commission according to Matthew, Jesus promises His presence to those who do His will. The presence of a person includes experiencing "His person", hearing the person's voice and enjoying the person's gifts.

As you are committed to obeying the Great Commission, you can expect to experience His person, enjoy His voice speaking to you all the time and also enjoy His gifts in your life. Many ministries do not have the presence of God any longer. They are very far from the Great Commission. This is why the church is powerless and no longer hears from God nor experiences His gifts and power.

7. THE GREAT COMMISSION IS A COMMISSION UNTIL THE END OF THE WORLD:

Jesus said, "Lo, I am with you alway, even unto the end of the world." This Great Commission is valid until the end of the world. No new commandment has been given to us. We are to carry on doing the same thing until the end of the world.

Some people think the Great Commission has already been fulfilled. How can this be when billions of people do not know Jesus Christ? How can you say the Great Commission has been fulfilled when the end of the world has not happened? This commission is till the end of the world.

Chapter 6

The Great Commission According to Mark

Afterward he appeared unto the eleven as they sat at meat, and upbraided them with their unbelief and hardness of heart, because they believed not them which had seen him after he was risen. And he said unto them, GO YE INTO ALL THE WORLD, AND PREACH THE GOSPEL TO EVERY CREATURE. HE THAT BELIEVETH AND IS BAPTIZED SHALL BE SAVED; BUT HE THAT BELIEVETH NOT SHALL BE DAMNED. AND THESE SIGNS shall follow them that believe; In my name shall they cast out devils; they shall speak with new tongues; They shall take up serpents; and if they drink any deadly thing, it shall not hurt them; they shall lay hands on the sick, and they shall recover. So then after the Lord had spoken unto them, he was received up into heaven, and sat on the right hand of God.

Mark 16:14-19

Marks' commission was given when Jesus appeared suddenly to the eleven whilst they were eating. This proves that God can give you a momentous message even whilst you are eating. Each and every one of the apostles repeated the Great Commission because they were the last words of Jesus Christ to us all.

According to Mark, these were the last words of Jesus Christ. They form what we call The Great Commission. These are the highlights of this Great Commission according to Mark. Let us look at Mark's Great Commission. Perhaps God will speak to you about an aspect of this Great Commission. Make yourselves saviours of men!

1. THE GREAT COMMISSION IS A COMMISSION TO GO:

Jesus said, "Go! Go!" These were His last words. These words have been disobeyed by a large percentage of the church.

The opposite of "going" is "staying"! The exact opposite of going somewhere is settling down. The exact opposite of going somewhere is establishing yourself somewhere else. What a nice and settled church we have today! There is very little movement, very little missionary work, very little evangelism and very little church planting.

What is the greatest characteristic of the present-day church? It is a church of pleasant feelings, pleasant meetings, pleasant songs, pleasant conferences and pleasant prospects. These are not people who want to go anywhere! These are not people that are going anywhere!

2. THE GREAT COMMISSION IS A COMMISSION TO SPECIFICALLY PREACH THE GOSPEL:

Jesus said, *"Preach the gospel!"* Unlike Matthew's commission, this commission specifies preaching and not teaching. Preach the good news of Jesus Christ! That is the gospel! "Gospel" means "good news." The news of Jesus Christ and the cross of Jesus Christ is the best news this world has ever heard.

Today, most pastors do not know how to preach the gospel. We can teach on prosperity, abundance, success, faith and miracles but few can actually preach the gospel.

I wrote a book called, "How you can Preach Salvation." I wrote that book because of the great deficiency in our preaching of the gospel. There are many ways in which you can preach the gospel. The gospel of Jesus Christ can be preached by preaching about the impending judgments of heaven and hell. The gospel of Jesus Christ can be preached by preaching about the love of God. You can preach about the blood of Jesus Christ. It is important for you to learn how to preach the gospel.

3. THE GREAT COMMISSION IS A COMMISSION TO GO TO ALL THE WORLD:

Jesus said, "Go ye into all the world!" This is the mandate we have been given. Who will go to *"all the world"*? The answer is "YOU will go to all the world!" Everyone thinks someone else will go to the entire world. That is why no one goes. You must assume a personal responsibility for this commission. You must think of the whole world. Your voice must be heard in the whole world. You must preach in the whole wide world.

4. THE GREAT COMMISSION IS A COMMISSION TO EVERY CREATURE:

Jesus said, "Preach ... to every creature!" Does that include animals? I do not think so. Souls lost in sin and depravity are like pitiful creatures that need help. The dying multitudes struggling in the ocean of desperation are the creatures Jesus is talking about.

The perishing crowds who live in sin, misery and pain are the creatures God is talking about. The thousands of shrieking, agonizing prostitutes, thieves, liars, blasphemers, drunkards, murderers and ungodly people are the creatures Jesus Christ is talking about. Many human beings are reduced to pitiful demonized creatures. Multitudes are thirsting for the milk of salvation.

5. THE GREAT COMMISSION IS A COMMISSION WITH SIGNS FOLLOWING:

Jesus said, "These signs shall follow [you]!" Expect these signs to follow you throughout your ministry:

Expect to speak with new tongues: Supernatural tongues will flow out of every great commissioner. Hours and hours of tongues must pour out of you. Tongues are a supernatural form of communication between you and heaven. Just as secret service personnel have radios for their secret and mysterious communication, you have been given tongues for your secret and mystical communication with heaven.

Expect to cast out devils: Demon spirits have occupied the masses. When you encounter a human being, you can assume you are encountering a demon power behind the person. We are dealing with demon spirits all the time.

Expect to survive the eating of poisonous and unhealthy things: Many of the things we eat today are not healthy. Because you are a gospel commissioner, you will not be harmed by anything that you eat or drink. Others may die from it, but you will survive!

Expect to survive life-threatening and dangerous events like taking up serpents: Others may die from it but you will not die. What kills others will not kill you because you are a great commissioner.

Expect to lay hands on the sick and expect the sick to recover: You become a powerful vessel of healing when you are a great commissioner. Do not underestimate your prayers. Your prayers will make people well. Your prayers will bring miracles to many people.

Chapter 7

The Great Commission According to Luke

And as they thus spake, Jesus himself stood in the midst of them, and saith unto them, Peace be unto you. But they were terrified and affrighted, and supposed that they had seen a spirit. And he said unto them, why are ye troubled? And why do thoughts arise in your hearts? Behold my hands and my feet, that it is I myself: handle me, and see; for a spirit hath not flesh and bones, as ye see me have. And when he had thus spoken, he shewed them his hands and his feet. And while they yet believed not for joy, and wondered, he said unto them, Have ye here any meat? And they gave him a piece of a broiled fish, and of an honeycomb. And he took it, and did eat before them. And he said unto them, These are the words which I spake unto you, while I was yet with you, that all things must be fulfilled, which were written in the law of Moses, and in the prophets, and in the psalms, concerning me.

Luke 24:36-44

THEN OPENED HE THEIR UNDERSTANDING, THAT THEY MIGHT UNDERSTAND THE SCRIPTURES, And said unto them, Thus it is written, and thus it behoved Christ to suffer, and to rise from the dead the third day: And THAT REPENTANCE AND REMISSION OF SINS SHOULD BE PREACHED IN HIS NAME AMONG ALL NATIONS, beginning at Jerusalem. And ye are witnesses of these things. And, behold, I send the promise of my Father upon you: but tarry ye in the city of Jerusalem, until ye be ENDUED WITH POWER from on high.

Luke 24:45-49

All the apostles repeated the last commission because they were the great commandments of Jesus Christ to us all. Let us look at this last commission in detail. Have you ever wondered why we do not meditate on the last words of Jesus Christ? This time, I believe God will speak to you about your role in world evangelism and church planting.

According to Luke, these were some of the last words of Jesus Christ. This commission was given in Jerusalem when Jesus appeared suddenly in the midst of His disciples.

These are the highlights of this Great Commission according to Luke. Make yourselves saviours of men!

1. THE GREAT COMMISSION IS A COMMISSION TO OPEN THE UNDERSTANDING OF PEOPLE:

Before giving the commission, Jesus opened their understanding to the scriptures. The scripture was made clear to them. Without the scripture being made clear to you, you will not give yourself to church planting and soul winning.

People whose understanding is not opened have developed a warped version of Christianity. Indeed, much of Christianity is simply the creation of human happiness, human excitement, pleasant interactions and pleasant socialization.

The Christian church without soul winning and church planting is a powerless, lifeless and aimless social club.

2. THE GREAT COMMISSION IS TO PREACH REPENTANCE:

The commission according to Luke, specifies the topics we are to preach about. Matthew and Mark do not specify the topics we are to preach about. In Luke's commission, we are clearly told to preach about repentance. Tell people to repent of their sins.

Repentance of sins means turning away from sin. The Great Commission includes the naming of the sins and wickedness of human beings so that they can turn away from them. Today, preachers do not mention sins in church. Sins like fornication, lying, stealing, and homosexuality are not mentioned any more. Mentioning the sin of homosexuality is called "hate speech." Because we do not preach about sin any more, the church is filled with unrepentant and unchanged religious sinners.

Jesus, in His last words to His disciples, mentioned the topic of repentance. How can we disregard a clear instruction given to the church? How can we ignore it and present ourselves as wise, self-righteous, dignified preachers?

Many pastors have become preachers of white lies.

A white lie is a lie that is told in order to be polite and to stop someone from being upset by the truth. Pastors are trying to be polite and prevent people from being upset. Are you called to be polite to the world? Did Jesus tell you to be polite? Did Jesus commission you to prevent people from being upset or offended? You are called to preach repentance. Stop making up stories and start preaching repentance!

3. THE GREAT COMMISSION IS A COMMISSION TO PREACH THE REMISSION OF SINS:

The Great Commission is the commission to preach about the forgiveness of sins. The blood of Jesus Christ washes away the sins of all those who come to the cross to receive mercy. To be a great commissioner, you must be an expert in preaching forgiveness and the remission of sins through the blood of Jesus.

To make yourselves saviours of men, you must be an expert in preaching about what Jesus Christ did on the cross for us. The cross of Jesus Christ at Calvary is the greatest event of forgiveness for the sins of our wicked world.

I once heard a pastor preaching about the cross. He said we are no longer to sing songs about hiding behind the cross. We are not cowards! We do not need to hide behind any cross! We are to sing songs about victory and abundance. It is no wonder that this minister withered and faded out of the ministry of Jesus Christ.

The words "Calvary", "the cross", "the blood" must not be made fun of. One pastor said he was glad that he no longer preached a religion of blood and the brutality of the cross. I watched as he ended his life and ministry in a rubbish dump. We must be wary of clever preaching that mocks at the foundations of Christianity.

We must be wary of these dignified and powerful ambassadors of the church who trivialise salvation, gospel preaching and make fun of the cross of Jesus Christ. If the cross of Jesus Christ is too basic for you, then you do not understand what Christianity is about.

We are commanded to preach the remission of sins. Let us do just that! We have not been commissioned to preach about finances and management planning. We have not been commissioned to preach about investments, politics, stocks and bonds. We have been commissioned to preach about the blood of Jesus Christ and the remission of sins.

4. THE GREAT COMMISSION IS A COMMISSION TO ALL NATIONS:

To be a great commissioner is to have an interest in all nations. Inward looking people are not interested in reaching the nations. People who are very nationalistic cannot be used to reach nations. Patriotism is good. It is good to shout slogans about your country. However, this patriotism has a way of excluding other nations.

I visited a great nation whose power extends across the globe. This nation is very patriotic, with the people being very proud to come from there. If you watch their TV programs, they say things like, "I thank God I was not born in Africa. I give glory to God that He spared me the agony of having to live in Africa." You will find that Christians in such "patriotic" countries do not fulfil the Great Commission.

Indeed, there is a large group of ministers who feel that they are fulfilling the Great Commission by going on television. They say, "I reach so many millions on TV every day." They say, "I am fulfilling the Great Commission to millions on television every day", when in actual fact no one is watching them.

No matter how much you are on television, you will have to send human beings to preach the gospel. There is no other way to preach the gospel than to go on the ground.

After Iraq was air-bombed by the United States, they still had to send ground troops if they wanted to win the war. No matter how many air strikes are delivered, the victory will be won when ground troops move in to take possession of the city.

5. THE GREAT COMMISSION IS A COMMISSION WITH THE POWER OF THE SPIRIT:

Jesus told them to wait for the power of the Holy Spirit. Indeed, the presence of the Holy Spirit is what you need to preach the gospel of Jesus Christ. Without the Holy Spirit's power you will preach economics, business, politics and maybe, even physics. It takes power to stay on the salvation trail. It takes power to preach about apparently abstract topics like the cross, Calvary and the blood of Jesus.

I heard one pastor make an unfortunate comment. He said, "What is the use of the blood, the cross and the nails to the people that I am preaching to? They need business! They need empowerment! They need success! They need to be successful in the marketplace!"

People who are against the cross of Jesus Christ should be driven out of the church because they are destroying the foundations of what we believe. Without power, you will find the gospel abstract and irrelevant. When you have the power of the Holy Spirit you will be able to stay on course and speak confidently about Jesus Christ even though He lived over two thousand years ago.

Chapter 8

The Great Commission According to John

This is now the third time that Jesus shewed himself to his disciples, after that he was risen from the dead. So when they had dined, Jesus saith to Simon Peter, Simon, son of Jonas, LOVEST THOU ME MORE THAN THESE? He saith unto him, Yea, Lord; thou knowest that I love thee. He saith unto him, feed my lambs. HE SAITH TO HIM AGAIN THE SECOND TIME, SIMON, SON OF JONAS, LOVEST THOU ME? HE SAITH UNTO HIM, YEA, LORD; THOU KNOWEST THAT I LOVE THEE. HE SAITH UNTO HIM, FEED MY SHEEP. HE SAITH UNTO HIM THE THIRD TIME, SIMON, SON OF JONAS, LOVEST THOU ME? Peter was grieved because he said unto him the third time, Lovest thou me? And he said unto him, Lord, thou knowest all things; thou knowest that I love thee. Jesus saith unto him, feed my sheep. Verily, verily, I say unto thee, when thou wast young, thou girdedst thyself, and walkedst whither thou wouldest: but when thou shalt be old, thou shalt stretch forth thy hands, and another shall gird thee, and carry thee whither thou wouldest not.

John 21:14-18

John repeats the last commission because it is the great commandment of Jesus Christ to us all. Let us look at this last commission in detail and meditate on the last words of Jesus Christ.

According to John, these were some of the last words of Jesus Christ. This event and this commissioning took place by the sea of Tiberias. These are the highlights of this Great Commission according to John. Make yourselves saviours of men!

1.   THE GREAT COMMISSION IS A COMMISSION OF LOVE:

Perhaps, your greatest expression of love to Jesus is to feed His sheep and to look after them. This is the Great Commission! Your great love for God can be expressed by feeding and teaching His little lambs.

The Great Commission is a commission of love. In this last chapter of the book of John, Jesus Christ spoke to Peter and commissioned him to feed His sheep and to teach them. There is a love element in this commission that is not found in any of the other three commissions. Love is therefore the highlight of the Great Commission according to John.

"Do you love me? If you love me feed my sheep." Feeding the sheep is the same as going to the nations. Feeding the sheep is the same as teaching the members. But Jesus is warning that only lovers of God will obey the Great Commission. How true this is!

Only those who love God can, and will obey the Great Commission. Today, it is as though there is a great commission to find money. It is as though the new great commission is to get rich and acquire the wealth of this world. Pastors preach as though they have been commissioned by God to make everyone rich. Perhaps, some people have a special instruction from the Lord to make people rich. But I am sure you cannot show me this great commission in the Bible. The Great Commission is the commission to preach the gospel. If you love God, you will obey him!

> He that hath my commandments, and keepeth them, he it
> is that loveth me: and he that loveth me shall be loved of
> my Father, and I will love him, and will manifest myself
> to him.
>
> John 14:21

When you have the commandment of God you obey Him and
you prove that you love Him. There is no other way to prove
that you love God. You cannot kiss God, you cannot love God,
you cannot have sex with God (excuse my language), you cannot
give God chocolate, you cannot write a letter to God. The only
way you can show God that you love Him is to obey Him. Jesus
said over and over that the only way to love Him was to obey
Him.

> Jesus answered and said unto him, If a man love me, he
> will keep my words: and my Father will love him, and we
> will come unto him, and make our abode with him.
>
> John 14:23

This reality must grip your heart today, Your failure to preach
the gospel and to obey the Great Commission is the greatest
evidence that you do not love God.

So if you do not love God, what do you love? You love what
you preach about. The topics that have filled your heart are the
things that you love. The money, the abundance, the prosperity
and the success are the things that you actually love. Out of the
abundance of your heart, your mouth is speaking all the time. It
is time to turn your heart towards God and to love God.

John was the baby disciple. He was the youngest and he
observed with great interest as Jesus asked Peter if he loved Him.
Today, the apostles are looking on with interest and amazement
at our lack of love for Jesus.

This is a commission to emphasise your love for God as the
basis of the Great Commission.

2. THE GREAT COMMISSION IS A COMMISSION TO FEED THE SHEEP:

In this version of the Great Commission, we see Jesus showing great love and concern for converts. The Great Commission includes following up of converts and teaching them the word of God. Teaching and repeating the words of Jesus Christ to converts is very important. Jesus really loves the people that are saved. He loves the souls that need salvation. He equally loves those that have come to know Him.

Your ability to care for people is a reflection of your understanding of the Great Commission. The Great Commission is not just the holding of a great crusade. A great crusade is a great achievement but is only a part of making yourself a saviour of men. I am a great believer in great crusades. But I am also a believer in church planting and caring for sheep. Being a good pastor and caring for the sheep is a vital part of being a great commissioner.

If you want to fulfil the Great Commission, you must develop your ability to have outreaches as well as care for the converts.

Chapter 9

The Great Commission According to Acts

And, being assembled together with them, commanded them that they should not depart from Jerusalem, but wait for the promise of the Father, which, saith he , ye have heard of me. For John truly baptized with water; but ye shall be baptized with the Holy Ghost not many days hence. When they therefore were come together, they asked of him, saying, Lord, wilt thou at this time restore again the kingdom to Israel? And he said unto them, It is not for you to know the times or the seasons, which the Father hath put in his own power. BUT YE SHALL RECEIVE POWER, AFTER THAT THE HOLY GHOST IS COME UPON YOU: AND YE SHALL BE WITNESSES UNTO ME BOTH IN JERUSALEM, AND IN ALL JUDAEA, AND IN SAMARIA, AND UNTO THE UTTERMOST PART OF THE EARTH. And when he had spoken these things, while they beheld, he was taken up; and a cloud received him out of their sight.

Acts 1:4-9

Luke repeats the last commission in the Book of Acts because it is the great commandment of Jesus Christ to us all. Let us look at this last commission in detail. Have you ever wondered why we do not meditate on the last words of Jesus Christ?

According to the Book of Acts these were the last words of Jesus Christ before He was taken up into glory from the Mount of Olives.

These last words of Jesus Christ are similar to the ones recorded in other books. This event and commission took place on the Mount of Olives (Acts 1:8-12). They form what we call The Great Commission. These are the highlights of this Great Commission according to the Book of Acts.

The highlights of this Great Commission are:

1. THE GREAT COMMISSION IS A COMMISSION DRIVEN BY THE HOLY SPIRIT:

A commission from the Holy Spirit: The highlight of this commission is the fact that the Holy Spirit is poured out into the world leading to an army of great commissioners being sent out. The direct response to the presence of the Holy Spirit is salvation and soul winning. Where the Holy Spirit is present, there is soul winning and there is an emphasis on the Great Commission. Where the Holy Spirit is absent, there is an emphasis on other things. Today, what do churches emphasize on? The church emphasizes on pleasant times, pleasant meetings, prosperity, security, safety, good living, good experiences, happiness, money, pleasant families, pleasant children, pleasant conferences and other nice events. Where the Holy Spirit has stopped working, people do not think of souls. A church devoid of the Holy Spirit is a church that has stopped planting churches and winning souls.

One day, the Lord showed me a church. Everyone's hands were lifted up as they worshipped the Lord. God spoke to me and said, "It is not my Spirit that is moving in this church. It is the spirit of the world." I was stunned. He told me it is the spirit of the world that loves the things of the world. The lust of the eyes, the lust of the flesh and the proud things of this life are all from the spirit of the world. He said to me, "Where the Holy Spirit is, there is soul winning, there is witnessing and there is the feeding of the sheep." A spirit cannot be seen! You can only see the evidence of the spirit. That is how the wind is. You cannot see the wind but you can see the evidence of the wind. The great evidence of the presence of the Holy Spirit is seen in the harvesting of the lost, perishing, agonizing and desperate multitudes to Jesus Christ.

2. THE GREAT COMMISSION IS A COMMISSION OF WITNESSING:

We have a commission to witness about Jesus Christ. In this commission, the unique element of witnessing is introduced. *The uniqueness of witnessing!*

Witnessing speaks of telling what you have seen and heard and experienced. This aspect of the Great Commission is unique because we are not given any topic to preach about. Witnessing is unique because every single person can be involved in the Great Commission. Your duty is to preach the gospel from a personal point of view. Your duty is to tell others what you have experienced from God. Suddenly, all of us can be involved in the Great Commission. The Great Commission is not the preserve of a great evangelist or a super-sacrificial missionary. God is expecting all who have experienced salvation to become commissioners.

What is involved in witnessing? What do witnesses do when they go to court? They simply say what they know and what they have seen. One night in London, I was awakened by the sound of an argument between a man and a woman. I looked out of the window and I saw a very angry man and a very angry woman having a heated argument. It must have been a relationship that had gone bad. Suddenly, the woman entered the house and slammed the door. The young man, very incensed, took his car and began ramming the building. He reversed his car at top speed into the house. The house literally trembled at the impact of the car being driven into the house. He did this several times and drove off. In a few minutes there were several police cars and flashing lights all over the area. A couple of days later, a policeman knocked on my door and asked if I had seen anything two nights earlier.

They wanted witnesses to come to the court to testify. Of course I excused myself and explained that I was just a visitor and did not live there. But what do you think they wanted me to say in court? Do you think they wanted me to preach the gospel? Do you think they wanted me to talk about anatomy, physiology and biochemistry?

Do you think they wanted me to talk about success, economics or how to become a millionaire? Certainly not! They just wanted me to share what I knew and what I had seen. That is what it means to be a witness. Everyone can be a witness. The policeman did not ask me for my education. I did not have to know anything about the law. I just had to say what I knew and what I had experienced.

The best commissioners are those who simply tell the story of how Jesus changed their lives. Everybody has a story. We have all done wrong and Jesus forgave us. But will you tell your story? Do you ever tell your story? It is time to encourage every single Christian to go out and tell the story of how Jesus Christ changed your life.

3. THE GREAT COMMISSION IS A COMMISSION IN FOUR PHASES:

This commission, according to the Book of Acts, has four clear phases. Unlike the earlier commissions that just told us to go to the whole world, this commission divides the mission into four clear phases: Jerusalem, Judea, Samaria and the uttermost parts of the earth.

The disciples started out in Jerusalem. Then they went to Judea, then to Samaria and then to the uttermost parts of the world.

Every ministry has four phases. If you fulfil your calling, you are likely to have four phases to your ministry. You will have a Jerusalem phase, a Judea phase, a Samaria phase and the uttermost parts of the earth phase. According to a vision that Kenneth Hagin had, most Christians do not even enter the first phase of their ministry. Are you going to enter the first phase of your ministry? Will you continue to the next phase of your ministry? Do you care about the souls that will perish because you do not obey God and enter the third phase of your ministry?

What about the uttermost parts of the earth? Will you ever go there? Will you ever do anything in those zones?

Jerusalem is your home base. Jerusalem is the beginning of your ministry. It is where salvation and ministry begins for you; your home city, your home country and your home community.

Judea is the very next major geographical area near you. If you started out in London, Judea is probably the rest of England, outside London. Judea is waiting for you to come there. You cannot praise yourself just because you have been successful in Jerusalem.

Samaria is even further than Judea. It is made up of people who are different from you. If you started out in London, Samaria is probably the rest of Europe. Samaria is equally waiting for you. People who are different from you will receive from you if you go to them. People who speak differently from you will receive from you if you care to talk to them. People who are a different colour from you will be saved if you open your mouth and talk about Jesus.

The uttermost parts of the earth are the furthermost parts of the earth from your starting point.

Today, most Christians start out in Jerusalem and end in Jerusalem. No one in Judea knows that you are saved. Samaria never benefits from the life that you have received. As for the uttermost parts of the earth, they are condemned to damnation as far as you are concerned. May God have mercy on us for not going through the four phases of the Great Commission.

4. THE GREAT COMMISSION IS A COMMISSION TO THE UTTERMOST CORNERS OF THE WORLD:

A highlight of the commission in the Book of Acts is the phrase "uttermost parts of the earth." The uttermost parts of the earth are the furthermost corners and the most remote islands of our world. There are many inhabited corners of this globe. It is the responsibility of the church to go to the inhabited corners of this globe.

Instead of finding out how to go there, pastors are involved in all kinds of business in the name of empowering modern day Christians in money and leadership. I hardly know of any modern day pastors who are discussing the uttermost and furthermost islands and locations of the earth. It is as though those corners of our inhabited globe are cursed. In fact, they are not cursed. It is the disobedient Christians who should watch out. God will find a way of reaching the lost agonizing creatures in our inhabited globe. I do not know how He is going to do it but I know He will find a way and He will find someone who will obey Him.

Many Christians say, "If God wants to get the gospel to an island, He will somehow get it to them or somehow bring the islanders to the gospel." If people like William Carey had followed such a low spiritual mentality, India would not have received the gospel.

I challenge you to rise up and put away the stupid spirit of disobedience and the nonsense Christianity of barrenness! It is time to start obeying the word of God and keeping the Great Commission. It is time to bear fruit.

Chapter 10

The Great Commission According to Timothy

I charge thee therefore before God, and the Lord Jesus Christ, who shall judge the quick and the dead at his appearing and his kingdom; PREACH THE WORD; BE INSTANT IN SEASON, OUT OF SEASON; reprove, rebuke, exhort with all longsuffering and doctrine. For the time will come when they will not endure sound doctrine; but after their own lusts shall they heap to themselves teachers, having itching ears; and they shall turn away their ears from the truth, and shall be turned unto fables. But watch thou in all things, endure afflictions, DO THE WORK OF AN EVANGELIST, make full proof of thy ministry. For I am now ready to be offered, and the time of my departure is at hand.

2 Timothy 4:1-6

A ll the apostles repeated the last commission because they were the great commandments of Jesus Christ to us all. Apostle Paul was also concerned about souls.

The apostle Paul had a son in the ministry called Timothy. Timothy is someone he gave instructions to. He poured out his heart and shared the word of God with him. At the very end of his life, he shared these last words with him. This is the Great Commission according to Paul!

How do I know that these were Apostle Paul's last words? They were his last words because they are in the last chapter of his letter to Timothy. They were his last words because as soon as he said, "Do the work of an evangelist," he informed Timothy that he was ready to die. "I am now ready to be offered", he said and "…the time of my departure is at hand." (2 Timothy 4:6)

What exactly were the last words of Paul to Timothy?

1.   THE GREAT COMMISSION IS A COMMISSION TO PREACH THE WORD OF GOD:

A commission to preach the word: Paul gave a commission to Timothy to preach the word of God. Today, many are preaching sermons that are more relevant in the university than in the church. God is calling us to become sound preachers of the word of God. Let us stick with hard, true scripture.

2.   THE GREAT COMMISSION IS A COMMISSION TO PREACH IN SEASON AND OUT OF SEASON:

A commission to preach in season and out of season: In season and out of season speaks of preaching at all times. There are only two possible times to preach; in season or out of season. Preaching out of season is preaching when it seems inappropriate. The time must come when preaching must be continuous and persistent. Preaching only on Sundays is an old tradition. God has taken us way beyond once-a-week preaching. Preaching must go on every day.

3. THE GREAT COMMISSION IS A COMMISSION TO GIVE SOUND DOCTRINE:

A commission to give sound doctrine: Sound doctrine speaks of things that are based on the Word. A lot of preaching is not sound. Stay with sound preaching and avoid false teachers. False teachers look just like good teachers. False teachers are real otherwise they would not be mentioned in the Bible. Do you know any false teachers? There are plenty around today.

4. THE GREAT COMMISSION IS A COMMISSION TO ENDURE AFFLICTIONS:

A commission to endure afflictions: Paul then gives a commission to endure afflictions and sufferings. The concepts of sacrifice, suffering and losing have been thrown out of the church. The apostle Paul, in his last words to Timothy, asked him to endure difficulties, afflictions and sufferings. He did not tell him to enjoy a good life, pleasant times, pleasant days, nice experiences and nice conferences. He warned him to endure and go through sufferings that he was destined to go through. Church planting will involve affliction and suffering. Church planting may involve sleeping on the floor for one year. Church planting may involve living in difficult towns and villages. Soul winning may involve risking your life to preach the gospel.

5. THE GREAT COMMISSION IS A COMMISSION TO DO THE WORK OF AN EVANGELIST AND TO MAKE FULL PROOF OF THE MINISTRY:

A commission do the work of an evangelist and make full proof of ministry: The very last words that Paul spoke to Timothy were "Do the work of an evangelist" and "fulfil your ministry." (2 Timothy 4:5, NASB)

These are truly great last words from a great person who walked with God. DO THE WORK OF AN EVANGELIST! DO THE WORK OF AN EVANGELIST! DO THE WORK OF AN EVANGELIST! DO THE WORK OF AN EVANGELIST!

These are the last words Paul declared before he informed Timothy of his impending death. It is amazing how the last words are the most important words. They contain the most important things of all.

You will notice how Paul did not speak to Timothy about his marriage. He did not tell Timothy that a good marriage was the most important thing for a minister. His last words were not about Timothy's business ventures. Paul's last words were not about having a good life or having nice times, nice experiences and nice friends.

Paul did not seem to emphasize human happiness and human achievements. His very last words were "do the work of an evangelist" and "fulfil your ministry". This must be the most important thing!

Care for the perishing souls! Think about the creatures in agony! Think about the drowning multitudes! Become an evangelist to the lost souls in the dark ocean of sin and wickedness! Share God with someone. God is real! He is alive! We shall all see Jesus one day and we shall know that telling people about Jesus was the most important thing a man could have done with his life!

Chapter 11

The Great Commission According to Jude

Keep yourselves in the love of God, looking for the mercy of our Lord Jesus Christ unto eternal life. And of some have compassion, making a difference: And others SAVE WITH FEAR, PULLING THEM OUT OF THE FIRE; HATING EVEN THE GARMENT SPOTTED BY THE FLESH. Now unto him that is able to keep you from falling, and to present you faultless before the presence of his glory with exceeding joy, To the only wise God our Saviour, be glory and majesty, dominion and power, both now and ever. Amen.

Jude 1:21-25

Ll the apostles repeated the last commission because they were the great commandments of Jesus Christ to us all.

In these very last words of Jude to the believers, you hear the voice of Jesus loud and clear. Jude has twenty-five verses that were accepted in the Bible. In the twenty-third verse he gave his last commission before giving praise to God. There were three clear segments of his great commission.

1. THE GREAT COMMISSION IS A COMMISSION TO SAVE PEOPLE WITH FEAR:

A commission to save people with fear: Save people with fear! You must be afraid of hell! You must be afraid of death because death is the end of life. There is no more opportunity to be saved after death. You must be afraid for people to go to hell.

You must be worried for their souls. You cannot just walk around in this world without being concerned about people who do not know God. Why do you think God saved you? Why do you think God showed you mercy and got you saved?

2. THE GREAT COMMISSION IS A COMMISSION TO PULL PEOPLE OUT OF FIRE:

A commission to pull people out of fire: There is a commission to pull people out of the fire. Which fire are we talking about? We are talking about the fires of hell. There are many people who are walking around who are virtually in hell. Many people have one foot in hell. Many people are a step away from death. Many people are about to die and go to hell.

The Great Commission is to snatch people from the fire. Someone may have one foot in hell but it is your duty to reach out and snatch them from hell fire. There are a lot of people on their deathbeds who will receive Christ. As they see eternity looming, they become more open to the gospel. Such people, who are half dead, only need someone who knows Jesus to snatch them out of the fire. They will give their lives to Jesus before they die. God is looking for people who will pull the half –dead and half-burnt souls out of the fire.

3. THE GREAT COMMISSION IS A COMMISSION NOT TO BE CONTAMINATED WITH SIN:

A commission to not be contaminated with sin: As you reach out to win the lost, Jude warns you not to be contaminated with sin. Contamination speaks of something you acquire because of your contact with it. Today, much of the church is worldly. The church is heavily contaminated with worldly visions and dreams. Much of the church is contaminated with the sin of idolatry. Idols of mammon are erected everywhere in the church.

Worldly visions of cars, wealth, diamonds, glitter, glamour, houses and money have contaminated the visions of God's servants. Men of God speak about worldly visions with greater passion than worldly CEOs and bank managers.

When someone is contaminated, it means he has the problem he is trying to save you from. When a doctor is contaminated with the Ebola virus, it means he has contracted the problem from his contact with the patient. Apostle Jude warns us not to be contaminated by the world we are trying to save. Unfortunately, this is exactly what has happened. God's servants are contaminated with the world. God's servants are truly contaminated with worldly pursuits and visions. This is why the church is no more becoming a saviour of men.

Apostle Jude's final words are words we must take seriously. We must get out of the contamination. We must make ourselves saviours of men!

Chapter 12

The Great Commission According to James

Elias was a man subject to like passions as we are, and he prayed earnestly that it might not rain: and it rained not on the earth by the space of three years and six months. And he prayed again, and the heaven gave rain, and the earth brought forth her fruit. Brethren, if any of you do err from the truth, and one convert him; LET HIM KNOW, THAT HE WHICH CONVERTETH THE SINNER FROM THE ERROR OF HIS WAY SHALL SAVE A SOUL FROM DEATH, AND SHALL HIDE A MULTITUDE OF SINS.

James 5:17-20

All the apostles repeated the last commission because they were the great commandments of Jesus Christ to us. Let us look at this last commission in detail. Have you ever wondered why Christians do not meditate on the last words of Jesus Christ? These are the highlights of this Great Commission according to James. Make yourselves saviours of men!

The Book of James has five chapters. The last chapter of James has twenty verses. The very last thing that James speaks about before signing out is the conversion of sinners from their sinful ways. The twentieth and last verse of the Book of James speaks of the conversion of sinners.

The conversion of sinners is the very last thing apostle James writes about. All through his letter, James speaks about wisdom, faith and many diverse topics. However, his last words have to do with the conversion of sinners and the saving of souls.

1. THE GREAT COMMISSION IS A COMMISSION FOR MEN WITH LIKE PASSIONS:

Apostle James points out that Elijah was a man with weaknesses and feelings just like all of us. In spite of this, God used him and answered his prayers. This is encouraging to all commissioners. Most commissioners can sense their own weaknesses and failings. Weaknesses and failings tend to discourage you from carrying out the Great Commission.

This is why Elijah's weaknesses are mentioned just before the parting words of James. This is to encourage all commissioners that you are just like Elijah. Keep pressing on in spite of the inflamed feelings and passions that you experience in your body. God is with you. He knows that he has sent weak men into the field. Supernatural power is needed to keep you on the Great Commission. You will have supernatural power and you will do wonders as you make yourselves saviours of men.

2. THE GREAT COMMISSION IS A COMMISSION TO CONVERT SINNERS:

Apostle James signs out of his book reminding everyone that the conversion of sinners saves souls. Make it your business to save souls. Make it your business to convert sinners and hide a multitude of sins. Is it not amazing that the apostles of Jesus Christ ended their messages in the same way?

Rescue the agonizing, shrieking, screaming souls from hell fire! Is it not amazing that James' last words are about the conversion of sinners! There is no mention of developing our happy human lives into a story of worldly success, prosperity and pleasantness. There is no mention of the market place, investments, stocks and Christian businesses. You can virtually hear Apostle James shouting, CONVERT A SINNER! CONVERT A SINNER! CONVERT A SINNER!

When you convert a sinner, you hide a multitude of sins. It may surprise you to note that you hide not only the sinner's sins but also your own sins. Pleasing God is not the art of sinless living. Pleasing God is the art of obedient living. There is none righteous. Even the most holy saints cannot claim purity before God. Your obedience to His commandments is your only chance of gaining favour with God.

Peter rejected it when people tried to honour him for healing the cripple. He said, "Do not think that it is by our own power or holiness that we have made this man to walk." (Acts 3:12) Peter knew that he had no personal holiness that he could boast of. He had already betrayed Christ and everyone knew it.

Obedience is your master key to pleasing God. We are hopeless sinners and failures, no matter how good we are. Isaiah found out the hard way that he was actually a foul-mouthed sinner! When God appeared to him, he screamed, "I am undone! I am a dirty man! I am a sinner! Everyone around me is a sinner!" (Isaiah 6:5)

What then can you do to improve your standing before God? The answer is obedience! If you love Him, obey Him! Obey Him with all your weaknesses. Carry yourself into His presence and seek to obey His precious commission to you. Do not try to be holy and perfect because you will not succeed. When you convert a sinner, you cover your own sins!

Indeed, when you convert a sinner you cover a multitude of sins. In the Book of Hebrews, all the heroes of faith were heroes because they believed and obeyed God. Not even one of them was clean before God. Prostitutes like Rahab, murderers like David, liars like Abraham and murderers like Moses all had the multitude of their sins covered through their obedience to God's commands. As you obey God and make yourself a savior of men your multitude of sins will be covered.

May God help us to become saviours of men!

Chapter 13

The Great Commission According to Peter

This second epistle, beloved, I now write unto you; in both which I stir up your pure minds by way of remembrance: That ye may be mindful of the words which were spoken before by the holy prophets, and of the commandment of us the apostles of the Lord and Saviour: Knowing this first, that there shall come in the last days scoffers, walking after their own lusts, And saying, Where is the promise of his coming? for since the fathers fell asleep, all things continue as they were from the beginning of the creation. For this they willingly are ignorant of, that by the word of God the heavens were of old, and the earth standing out of the water and in the water: Whereby the world that then was, being overflowed with water, perished: BUT THE HEAVENS AND THE EARTH, WHICH ARE NOW, BY THE SAME WORD ARE KEPT IN STORE, RESERVED UNTO FIRE AGAINST THE DAY OF JUDGMENT AND PERDITION OF UNGODLY MEN.   But, beloved, be not ignorant of this one thing, that one day is with the Lord as a thousand years, and a thousand years as one day. THE LORD IS NOT SLACK CONCERNING HIS

PROMISE, AS SOME MEN COUNT SLACKNESS; BUT IS LONGSUFFERING TO US-WARD, NOT WILLING THAT ANY SHOULD PERISH, BUT THAT ALL SHOULD COME TO REPENTANCE. BUT THE DAY OF THE LORD WILL COME AS A THIEF IN THE NIGHT; in the which the heavens shall pass away with a great noise, and the elements shall melt with fervent heat, the earth also and the works that are therein shall be burned up. Seeing then that all these things shall be dissolved, what manner of persons ought ye to be in all holy conversation and godliness, LOOKING FOR AND HASTING UNTO THE COMING OF THE DAY OF GOD, wherein the heavens being on fire shall be dissolved, and the elements shall melt with fervent heat? Nevertheless we, according to his promise, look for new heavens and a new earth, wherein dwelleth righteousness. Wherefore, beloved, seeing that ye look for such things, be diligent that ye may be found of him in peace, without spot, and blameless. And account that the longsuffering of our Lord is salvation; even as our beloved brother Paul also according to the wisdom given unto him hath written unto you;

2 Peter 3:1-15

All the apostles repeated the last commission because they were the great commandments of Jesus Christ to us all. Let us look at the last commission given by the apostle Peter. I believe the apostles meditated on the last words of Jesus. The last words of Peter are found in the last words of the second letter of Peter. In these words again, you find the emphasis falling squarely on soul winning.

Let us have a look at the highlights of this Great Commission according to Peter.

1. THE GREAT COMMISSION IS A COMMISSION TO ENSURE THAT NONE WILL PERISH:

Peter's last words are a commission to understand the looming judgments of God. Peter clearly declares that people are willingly ignorant of the fact that God is going to burn the earth with fire. These thoughts must be in the heart of every commissioner. Fire is coming! Judgment is coming!

Every great commissioner must believe that God is not willing that any should perish. It is amazing that Peter, in his last words, will speak about the fact that God did not want anyone to perish or go to hell.

Is that not why Jesus said we should go to the ends of the world? Is that not why Jesus said we should go to the uttermost parts of the world? God does not want anyone to perish even if they live in the uttermost part of the world.

God does not want anyone to perish even if they live on an island. God loves the whole world dearly. Will you love what He loves?

Will you care for what He cares for?

2. THE GREAT COMMISSION IS A COMMISSION TO PREPARE THE WORLD FOR A SUDDEN AND UNEXPECTED JUDGEMENT:

It is our duty as great commissioners to prepare the world for a sudden and unexpected judgment. The day of the Lord will come as a thief in the night... (2 Peter 3:10). Do thieves announce their arrival? Certainly not!

Jesus compared Himself with the coming of a thief. You must understand how sudden and unexpected His judgment of this world is going to be. It is time for you to go out and warn people of a sudden change that is going to come into the world.

There are two ways in which a sudden and unexpected judgment is going to come. One way is to die. Most people are surprised when they die. They are alive one day; then they find they are unable to do what they used to do. I remember a lady who was travelling abroad for a concert. She had bought her plane ticket and had millions of fans lined up for her programs. But she died suddenly in an accident the night before she could leave. She must have been surprised that she was not in the countries she had planned to perform in. She was suddenly in a place where all her plans, purposes and pursuits were no more.

Judgment day will come to every single human being on the earth. The problem is that these dates have not been revealed to us. This is what makes our commission even more urgent. We must rush out there and inform people that judgment day is coming. Judgment day may be very unexpected.

The second way in which sudden and unexpected judgment will come is through the return of the Lord Jesus Christ. Jesus will return any day from now. There is enough confusion in the world that warrants the appearance of a Saviour. There are so many volcanoes, wars, earthquakes and rumours of wars, to prove that it may be time for Jesus to return.

Many of the prophecies of Jesus have been fulfilled. No one can tell exactly when Jesus will return. It may be in my lifetime; it may be in yours! The Great Commission according to Peter is to prepare the world for a sudden and abrupt ending to everything.

3. THE GREAT COMMISSION IS A COMMISSION TO HASTEN THE COMING OF THE LORD:

The last commission of Peter is to hasten the coming of the Lord. *"Looking for and hasting unto the coming of the day of God, wherein the heavens being on fire shall be dissolved, and the elements shall melt with fervent heat?"* How do you hasten the coming of the Lord? By evangelism! Jesus prophesied that wars, rumours of wars and confusion would not be enough to provoke the coming of the Lord. He said the gospel will be preached to the ends of the world and then the end would come.

And this gospel of the kingdom shall be preached in all the world for a witness unto all nations; and then shall the end come.

Matthew 24:14

Peter's last words in the last chapter of his last book tell us to hasten the coming of the Lord. Indeed, we are called to hasten the coming of the Lord by preaching with all our strength and with all our might.

Let us go out there and do what we can. Let us plant churches! Let us win souls! Let us snatch the sinners from hell fire! It is the Great Commission. It is our commission! It is Jesus' commission to us!

Let us show Him that we love Him. Let us show Him that we believe in Him. Let us go to the ends of the world. Let us stop preaching about secular things! Let us preach the word of God!

Chapter 14

The Great Commission According to Revelation

And, behold, I come quickly; and my reward is with me, to give every man according as his work shall be. I am Alpha and Omega, the beginning and the end, the first and the last. Blessed are they that do his commandments, that they may have right to the tree of life, and may enter in through the gates into the city. For without are dogs, and sorcerers, and whoremongers, and murderers, and idolaters, and whosoever loveth and maketh a lie. I Jesus have sent mine angel to testify unto you these things in the churches. I am the root and the offspring of David, and the bright and morning star. AND THE SPIRIT AND THE BRIDE SAY, COME. AND LET HIM THAT HEARETH SAY, COME. AND LET HIM THAT IS ATHIRST COME. AND WHOSOEVER WILL, LET HIM TAKE THE WATER OF LIFE FREELY. For I testify unto every man that heareth the words of the prophecy of this book, If any man shall add unto these things, God shall add unto him the plagues that are written in this book: AND IF ANY MAN SHALL TAKE AWAY FROM THE WORDS OF THE BOOK OF THIS PROPHECY, GOD SHALL TAKE AWAY

HIS PART OUT OF THE BOOK OF LIFE, and out of the holy city, and from the things which are written in this book. He which testifieth these things saith, Surely I come quickly. Amen. Even so, come, Lord Jesus. The grace of our Lord Jesus Christ be with you all. Amen.

Revelation 22:12-21

A s the Bible closes in its last chapter and its last few words, we hear the Holy Spirit speak. The bride of Jesus Christ is the true church of Jesus Christ. Both the Holy Spirit and the true church say the same thing: Come to God! "Make yourselves saviours of men" is a message from the Holy Spirit.

1.   THE GREAT COMMISSION IS A LAST WORD FROM THE HOLY SPIRIT:

It is interesting that the last words in the Book of Revelation are so clear; "Come." As the Book of Revelation closes what are the last words to the world? "COME!" "COME!" "COME!" "COME!"

Come and do what? Come and drink of the water of life freely! Come and enjoy salvation! Come to God! Come to Jesus! These are the words of the Holy Spirit inviting the poor, agonizing, shrieking, screaming, frightened, desperate creatures and souls in this world. Come out of the dark ocean and into the love of God.

2.   THE GREAT COMMISSION IS A LAST WORD FROM THE TRUE BRIDE:

The commission of the true church, the words of the true bride of Jesus are clear; COME! COME! COME! COME! The true church is always inviting people to God. The true church is always inviting people to come to Jesus. The false church is always celebrating and having pleasant times with pleasant people on pleasant occasions. The false church has no such message.

The false church says, STAY HERE! SETTLE DOWN! CELEBRATE! PROSPER TODAY! SECURE YOURSELF! ENRICH YOURSELF! MAKE YOURSELF HAPPY!

Today, you must ask yourself, "Are the last words of Jesus important to me?" Are the last words of the Holy Spirit important to you? Did you know that His last words were "COME"?

Are the last words of the true bride important to you? Did you know that the true bride is evangelizing the world and saying to the whole world, COME TO GOD? Did you know that the false bride is saying something completely different? The false bride is saying, "Relax, take it easy, have fun, things are getting better for believers!"

It is time for us to make ourselves saviours of men. It is time to believe the word of God. It is time to set aside the nonsense that is being preached instead of the gospel. The Great Commission must become our passion again! The Great Commission and words of Jesus must possess our hearts again! Making ourselves saviours of men must be our foremost mission.

In Conclusion

Let us give ourselves to this glorious mission unreservedly. Let us never think that our time, our strength, our families are our own.

Let us dedicate them all to God and to His work. Let us give ourselves wholly that our profiting may appear.

Are we justified in staying here while so many are perishing without means of grace in other lands? We must take every chance of doing good to the lost. We will be labouring, we will be travelling day and night!

We must instruct, we must teach, exhort, rebuke and preach the word.

With all long suffering and an anxious desire for the lost.

We must be instant in prayer for the pouring out of the sweet Holy Spirit upon all the people. Surely, it is worthwhile to push ourselves with all our might in promoting the gospel and the kingdom of our Christ.

Dear friends, God is gracious! Do not run away from Him!

A few more days, and our work down here will be done!

When it's done, it's done for eternity!

Your life spent is irrevocable and it remains to be contemplated through all eternity!

References

Excerpts taken from

Chapter 1

"*Commentary on Romans*", Charles Spurgeon, Titus Books, 2014 Retrieved from: http://www.truthmagazine.com/archives/volume38/GOT038307.html 10 April 2019

Chapter 4

"*Who Cares?*" by General William Booth Retrieved from: https://revpacman.wordpress.com/2017/09/16/who-cares-general-william-booth/ 10 April 2019

Chapter 6

"*Who Cares?*" by General William Booth Retrieved from: https://revpacman.wordpress.com/2017/09/16/who-cares-general-william-booth/ 10 April 2019

Chapter 7

"*White-lie*" definition Retrieved from: https://dictionary.cambridge.org/dictionary/english/white-lie 10 April 2019

Chapter 9

What is God like? – Is there a God? Retrieved from: https://www.isthereagod.com.au/index.php/what-is-god-like 10 April 2019

Chapter 11

Locusts in Tribulation Retrieved from https://hopeofisrael.net/news/demonic-locusts-torment-people-worldwide/ 10 April 2019

Chapter 14

William Carey, *An Enquiry into the Obligations of Christians to Use Means for the Conversion of the Heathens*, First Published 1792

Labour to be

Blessed

...labour not to be rich

DAG HEWARD-MILLS

Parchment House

Unless otherwise stated, all Scripture quotations are taken from the King James Version of the Bible.

LABOUR TO BE BLESSED...*LABOUR NOT TO BE RICH*

Copyright © 2017 Dag Heward-Mills

First Edition published by Parchment House 2019
1st Printing 2019

[77]Find out more about Dag Heward-Mills
Healing Jesus Crusade
Write to: evangelist@daghewardmills.org
Website: www.daghewardmills.org
Facebook: Dag Heward-Mills
Twitter: @EvangelistDag

ISBN: 978-1-64329-217-5

Contents

CHAPTER 1

Labour to be Blessed!

There is one alone, and there is not a second; yea, he hath neither child nor brother: yet is there no end of all his labour; neither is his eye satisfied with riches; NEITHER SAITH HE, FOR WHOM DO I LABOUR, AND BEREAVE MY SOUL OF GOOD? This is also vanity, yea, it is a sore travail.

Ecclesiastes 4:8

S olomon, the wisest man to ever live, made an observation that we must consider deeply. He wondered why people were working endlessly. He wondered if people asked themselves why they were so bent on fighting, labouring, suffering, working and sweating in this world. Perhaps, these are some of the questions that Wisdom is asking you today.

1. What are you in school for?

2. What are you working for?

3. What are you sweating for?

4. What are you struggling about?

5. What are you building for?

6. What are you travelling for?

7. What are you migrating for?

8. What are you sacrificing for?

9. What are you labouring day and night for?

10. What are you fighting for?

11. What are you suffering for?

12. What are you dying for?

These are also questions that come into my mind whenever I see people struggling, hustling, working and suffering in our dark and difficult world. Many people achieve their goals several times over but still do not know why they are working. Many people acquire houses, cars and lands that they cannot even use. To what purpose are all these acquisitions? What makes men go on and on, working for money that they will not use?

I met a businessman who was working so hard. He had achieved so many things in this life. He had a car! He had houses! He had money! And he had more contracts than he could handle. I was wondering what he was trying to achieve. What was in his mind as he continued to struggle, sweat and suffer? To what purpose were all his efforts? So I asked this businessman why he was working so hard. He said he just wanted more and more of the same things. He wanted to be richer than he was. He was wealthier than most people I knew. Yet, he wanted more, and more and more!

Most people do not think about what they are doing. Most men are engaged in a fight for something. Some imaginary goal is set before them and they labour on mindlessly!

Is it not amazing to you that there is a scripture that states that we should not labour to be rich? In other words, labouring for riches is not a wise thing to do.

If we are not labouring to be rich, then what are we labouring for? Is there any other goal or purpose that we can give ourselves to?

Is there any other good reason for working, struggling, suffering, sweating and labouring night and day?

Is there any other good reason for all the jobs we take up and all the sacrifices we make at work every day?

Yes, there can be a good reason for all your work! God has given us something good to fight for. "Fight the good fight" is what the bible says! In other words, there are fights that are not good fights. There are fights that are not worth fighting.

So what is there that is worth fighting for? What is there that is worth my time, my life, my suffering, my sweating and my struggles? Does everyone have to become a full time priest? Are you saying that I should stop working and become a priest because there is no point in working? No, that is not what I am saying! God does not expect everyone to become a priest. Most people will not become priests. Even in the Old Testament the full time Levites who did not do ordinary work were in the minority. The majority of the tribes of Israel were normal workers in the society.

This is not a book about becoming a full time pastor. This message is about carrying on as a businessman, a worker and a professional who has a good purpose for all his work.

I do not want you to be a purposeless businessman or professional. I do not want you to have the wrong purpose or vision as you work. Labour not to be rich! Do not have a vision to be rich. Have a vision to be blessed!

Your vision must be to obtain a blessing rather than to obtain riches. Instead of fighting for money, fight for a blessing. A blessing is what will change your life. Jacob and Esau wrestled over a blessing. Jacob and Esau did not fight over money. They fought over a blessing. Each of them wanted to be blessed. At the end of this fight, Jacob obtained the blessing. Jacob is Israel and Israel is one of the richest and most successful groups of people on earth today. It is a far greater purpose for you to desire a blessing and work for a blessing than to desire and work for riches. Learn from the example of Jacob and Esau. Fight for blessings rather than for money! Fight to be a blessed person. Live your whole life seeking, fighting, struggling, sweating, working and forcing to acquire a blessing. Do whatever it takes to obtain a blessing on your life. As you read this book, you will receive revelation on how to live your life to receive a blessing.

And Rebekah heard when Isaac spake to Esau his son. And Esau went to the field to hunt for venison, and to bring it.

And Rebekah spake unto Jacob her son, saying, Behold, I heard thy father speak unto Esau thy brother, saying, Bring me venison, and make me savoury meat, that I may eat, and bless thee before the Lord before my death. Now therefore, my son, obey my voice according to that which I command thee. Go now to the flock, and fetch me from thence two good kids of the goats; and I will make them savoury meat for thy father, such as he loveth: And thou shalt bring it to thy father, that he may eat, and that he may bless thee before his death. And Jacob said to Rebekah his mother, Behold, Esau my brother is a hairy man, and I am a smooth man: My father peradventure will feel me, and

I shall seem to him as a deceiver; and I shall bring a curse upon me, and not a blessing. And his mother said unto him, Upon me be thy curse, my son: only obey my voice, and go fetch me them. And he went, and fetched, and brought them to his mother: and his mother made savoury meat, such as his father loved.

Genesis 27:5-14

CHAPTER 2

Labour Not to be Rich

Labour not to be rich: ...

Proverbs 23:4

Most people want to be rich! Most people are working because they want to be rich. Most people are labouring day and night so that they become rich. Yet the scripture says, "Labour not to be rich." Labour not to be rich is a clear instruction from the Lord!

If you should not labour to be rich, what should you do? Why are we working if we are not trying to be rich? What should a businessman do? Should he not try to be rich? What should he do? Why should a man not aim to be wealthy? Because God's word says so!

This book is about what you must give your life to. Indeed, there are things you can aim for and labour for other than riches. This book is going to tell you what your vision can be. Instead of trying to be rich, you will learn to labour for other things.

It is not a wise thing for you to aim to be rich because God's word says so. God wants to give you a better vision for your life. Instead of labouring to be rich, it is better for you to labour to be blessed and to labour to be a blessing.

The scripture says, we should stop trying to be wiser than God. Cease from your own wisdom and "do not labour to be rich".

Labour not to be rich: cease from thine own wisdom.

Proverbs 23:4

After reading this book you will have a new vision. Your vision will not be to become a rich person. Your vision will be to become a person who is blessed by God. Your vision will be to become a blessing to others!

The blessing of the Lord is what you need. Within the blessing of the Lord, you will have more than enough and to spare. You must always ask yourself "Why am I working? What am I working for? What do I want to achieve? Do I want to pile up riches so that I can stare at them and praise myself?"

"How much can I eat? What will I do with all these things I am trying to acquire? What price do I have to pay to have all these riches? Am I going to sacrifice my very life to be rich? Am I going to throw away God so that I can have riches? Do I want to join the multitudes who were not able to enter the kingdom of heaven because of money? Do I want to be a rich fool or do I want to be a blessed person?"

And he spake a parable unto them, saying, the ground of a certain rich man brought forth plentifully: And he thought within himself, saying, What shall I do, because I have no room where to bestow my fruits? And he said, this will I do: I will pull down my barns, and build greater; and there will I bestow all my fruits and my goods. And I will say to my soul, Soul, thou hast much goods laid up for many years; take thine ease, eat, drink, and be merry. But God said unto him, Thou fool, this night thy soul shall be required of thee: then whose shall those things be, which thou hast provided? SO IS HE THAT LAYETH UP TREASURE FOR HIMSELF, AND IS NOT RICH TOWARD GOD.

Luke 12:16-21

You must labour to be blessed because the blessings of the Lord make you rich and there is no sorrow added to it. There are reasons why God's word teaches us not to labour to be rich. Riches have several characteristics that make them a dangerous goal for anyone. Here are some of the clear biblical warnings about the nature of riches and why they must not be your life's vision.

1. **Labour not to be rich because ill-gotten riches can cut your life short. Those who get riches but not in the right way, can have their life cut short.**

I the Lord search the heart, I try the reins, even to give every man according to his ways, and according to the fruit of his doings. As the partridge sitteth on eggs, and hatcheth them not; so HE THAT GETTETH RICHES, AND NOT

BY RIGHT, SHALL LEAVE THEM IN THE MIDST OF HIS DAYS, and at his end shall be a fool.

Jeremiah 17:10-11

2. Labour not to be rich because earthly riches can turn you into a fool.

And he said unto them, Take heed, and beware of covetousness: for a man's life consisteth not in the abundance of the things which he possesseth. And he spake a parable unto them, saying, the ground of a certain rich man brought forth plentifully: And he thought within himself, saying, what shall I do, because I have no room where to bestow my fruits? And he said, this will I do: I will pull down my barns, and build greater; and there will I bestow all my fruits and my goods. And I will say to my soul, Soul, thou hast much goods laid up for many years; take thine ease, eat, drink, and be merry. BUT GOD SAID UNTO HIM, THOU FOOL, THIS NIGHT THY SOUL SHALL BE REQUIRED OF THEE: THEN WHOSE SHALL THOSE THINGS BE, WHICH THOU HAST PROVIDED? So is he that layeth up treasure for himself, and is not rich toward God.

Luke 12:15-21

3. Labour not to be rich because riches can prevent you from taking up your cross and following Jesus. Riches can prevent you from entering the kingdom of God.

And when he was gone forth into the way, there came one running, and kneeled to him, and asked him, Good Master, what shall I do that I may inherit eternal life? And Jesus said unto him, Why callest thou me good? There is none good but one, that is, God. Thou knowest the commandments, Do not commit adultery, Do not kill, Do not steal, Do not bear false witness, Defraud not, Honour thy father and mother. And he answered and said unto him, Master, all these have I observed from my youth. Then Jesus beholding him loved him, and said unto him,

9

One thing thou lackest: go thy way, sell whatsoever thou hast, and give to the poor, and thou shalt have treasure in heaven: and come, take up the cross, and follow me. And he was sad at that saying, and went away grieved: for he had great possessions. And JESUS LOOKED ROUND ABOUT, AND SAITH UNTO HIS DISCIPLES, HOW HARDLY SHALL THEY THAT HAVE RICHES ENTER INTO THE KINGDOM OF GOD!

Mark 10:17-23

4. Labour not to be rich because riches are deceptive and can deceive you.

And the cares of this world, and the DECEITFULNESS OF RICHES, and the lusts of other things entering in, choke the word, and it becometh unfruitful.

Mark 4:19

5. Labour not to be rich because riches are unrighteous mammon. Unrighteous mammon is not the same as true riches.

If therefore ye have not been faithful in the UNRIGHTEOUS MAMMON, who will commit to your trust the true riches?

Luke 16:11

6. Labour not to be rich because riches can choke the word of God. Riches can drown the word of God and the message of God in your life. The word of God in your life is also the call of God. Riches can drown the call of God on your life. This is why many rich people do not follow the call of God. It is not that God does not call rich and successful people. He calls them but the Word is choked by the riches.

And that which fell among thorns are they, which, when they have heard, go forth, and are CHOKED WITH CARES AND RICHES and pleasures of this life, and bring no fruit to perfection.

Luke 8:14

7. **Labour not to be rich because riches are uncertain things.** Why should you spend your life struggling to get something that is uncertain and unpredictable? Wealth is a very uncertain and unpredictable thing. Your wealth can be taken up by a flood, an earthquake or some other financial or personal crisis. Many people whom we see as wealthy are actually in financial crises. They are under so much pressure because of their debts and other uncertainties.

Charge them that are rich in this world, that they be not highminded, nor trust in UNCERTAIN RICHES, but in the living God, who giveth us richly all things to enjoy;

1 Timothy 6:17

8. **Labour not to be rich because riches are often corrupted and polluted with some kind of evil.** Most riches have an evil source. A lot of wealth has grown out of the sins and crimes committed by our ancestors. Many people have slave traders as their ancestors! Many people have criminals as their ancestors! Many people have thieves as their ancestors! Many people have murderers as their ancestors! Much of the wealth of this world has its foundation in evil. The word of God is teaching us not to spend our lives searching for this corrupted wealth.

Go to now, ye rich men, weep and howl for your miseries that shall come upon you. YOUR RICHES ARE CORRUPTED, and your garments are motheaten. Your gold and silver is cankered; and the rust of them shall be a witness against you, and shall eat your flesh as it were fire. Ye have heaped treasure together for the last days. Behold, the hire of the labourers who have reaped down your fields, which is of you kept back by fraud, crieth: and the cries of them which have reaped are entered into the ears of the Lord of sabaoth.

James 5:1-4

11

9. **Labour not to be rich because riches can make you very proud. God resists the proud (James 4:6).** Why should you spend your life labouring for something that will most likely make you proud? Why should you spend your life labouring for something that will make God resist you and fight against you?

With thy wisdom and with thine understanding thou hast gotten thee riches, and hast gotten gold and silver into thy treasures: By thy great wisdom and by thy traffick hast thou increased thy riches, and THINE HEART IS LIFTED UP BECAUSE OF THY RICHES:

Ezekiel 28:4-5

10. **Labour not to be rich because riches can hurt you.** Riches can harm you! Giving money to someone can destroy him. The prodigal son's money destroyed him.

There is a sore evil which I have seen under the sun, namely , RICHES KEPT FOR THE OWNERS THEREOF TO THEIR HURT.

Ecclesiastes 5:13

11. **Labour not to be rich because riches are hidden and will require your whole life to find them.**

And I will give thee the treasures of darkness, and hidden riches of secret places, that thou mayest know that I, the Lord, which call thee by thy name, am the God of Israel.

Isaiah 45:3

12. **Labour not to be rich because riches are often unusable. Riches are often never really enjoyed by their owners. Why is this?** Many rich people are unhappy. Many rich people have bad marriages and difficult relationships. Many rich people have warped personal lives.

Research has shown that earning more than a certain amount of money does not change your life significantly. For instance, having seventeen toilets and bathrooms instead of three toilets and bathrooms in your house will not change your life much. You simply cannot use the extra toilets and bathrooms in your house all at once. Therefore your life does not change much with the extra toilets and bathrooms.

A man to whom God hath given riches, wealth, and honour, so that he wanteth nothing for his soul of all that he desireth, yet God giveth him not power to eat thereof, but a stranger eateth it: this is vanity, and it is an evil disease.

Ecclesiastes 6:2

13. Labour not to be rich because riches are unstable. Riches do not stay for long. Riches tend to go away from their owners. You have to do a lot to retain your wealth.

Wilt thou set thine eyes upon that which is not? for riches certainly make themselves wings; they fly away as an eagle toward heaven.

Proverbs 23:5

14. Labour not to be rich because you will never be satisfied by riches. Rich people are some of the most discontented and unhappy people. They seem to have everything and yet they are constantly in search of something else. This is why so many wealthy celebrities are drug addicts and alcoholics. They are looking for something to satisfy them. Nothing can satisfy you except Jesus!

He that loveth silver shall not be satisfied with silver; nor he that loveth abundance with increase: this is also vanity.

Ecclesiastes 5:10

15. Labour not to be rich because you are just working for others. Do you think that Steve Jobs enjoyed life much more than you, or Bill Gates for that matter? These people have simply created wealth and jobs for many others all over the world. Apart from staring at your mountain of riches, there is very little your riches can do for you. Indeed, the scripture is full of wisdom for those who are seeking after riches and wealth.

When goods increase, they are increased that eat them: and what good is there to the owners thereof, saving the beholding of them with their eyes?

Ecclesiastes 5:11

16. Labour not to be rich because you are labouring for the wind. Most riches are for the wind; to be blown away into nothingness. Labour rather to be blessed!

But those riches perish by evil travail: and he begetteth a son, and there is nothing in his hand. As he came forth of his mother's womb, naked shall he return to go as he came, and shall take nothing of his labour, which he may carry away in his hand. And this also is a sore evil, that in all points as he came, so shall he go: and what profit hath he that hath laboured for the wind?

Ecclesiastes 5:14-16

17. Labour not to be rich because riches are linked to many temptations and traps. Labouring blindly for these riches will lead you to many evils and temptations. Labouring for riches is like labouring for a temptation. It is as though you are shouting, "I want a temptation! I want a snare to fall upon me! Somebody should please set a trap for me!" This is why the scripture says, "Labour not to be rich."

BUT THEY THAT WILL BE RICH FALL INTO TEMPTATION AND A SNARE, and into many foolish and hurtful lusts, which drown men in destruction and perdition. For the love of money is the root of all evil: which while some coveted after, they have erred from the faith, and pierced themselves through with many sorrows.

1 Timothy 6:9-10

14

18. Labour not to be rich because riches are laden with foolish and hurtful desires.

BUT THEY THAT WILL BE RICH fall into temptation and a snare, and INTO MANY FOOLISH AND HURTFUL LUSTS, which drown men in destruction and perdition. For the love of money is the root of all evil: which while some coveted after, they have erred from the faith, and pierced themselves through with many sorrows.

1 Timothy 6:9-10

19. Labour not to be rich because they that aim to be rich are drowned in destruction and perdition. The scriptures are clear on what happens to those who labour for the riches of this world.

BUT THEY THAT WILL BE RICH fall into temptation and a snare, and into many foolish and hurtful lusts, which DROWN MEN IN DESTRUCTION AND PERDITION. For the love of money is the root of all evil: which while some coveted after, they have erred from the faith, and pierced themselves through with many sorrows.

1 Timothy 6:9-10

CHAPTER 3

What is in a Blessing?

Blessings are powerful in their very nature. They have inherent powers that affect human life. There is no way to explain human life except you accept that blessings and curses are real. Blessings are a mystical force behind human existence. You will succeed in this life through the blessings that are spoken over your life. When you go to church, you will receive some teachings, you may write some notes and you may learn some good things. But what you really need is the blessing of the Lord.

The first thing that God did for human beings, after He created them, was to bless them. Jacob did not seek to write notes to remember his father's wisdom. He simply wanted a blessing from his father. Can you imagine two brothers, Jacob and Esau, quarrelling over blessings? They were not quarrelling over money or property. They were not asking each other, "How much money did you get? What did he give you for your birthday?" These were not brothers who were quarrelling over an inheritance. Jacob and Esau were brothers who fought over spoken blessings.

Joseph prevailed because of the blessings that were on his life. The scripture says the blessings of his father prevailed (Genesis 49:26).

People will acknowledge you because of the blessings that are operating in your life and not because of the notes you wrote in class.

Isaiah prophesied that people would be forced to acknowledge you because of the blessing in your life. They would just take one look at you and say, "This is the seed God has blessed." "And their seed shall be known among the Gentiles, and their offspring among the people: ALL THAT SEE THEM SHALL ACKNOWLEDGE THEM, THAT THEY ARE THE SEED WHICH THE LORD HATH BLESSED" (Isaiah 61:9).

When Isaac discovered that he had mistakenly blessed the wrong person, he simply said, "I have mistakenly made him your lord, I have sustained him with my blessings."

Jacob received those blessings from his father Isaac. It is those blessings that are sustaining Israel today. It is those blessings that are causing them to have more inventors, scientists and billionaires than any other nation.

You may try but you will not find any other reason to explain why this group of people are as unusually blessed as they are.

1. YOU SUCCEED IN LIFE BY BLESSINGS.

And when Esau heard the words of his father, he cried with a great and exceeding bitter cry, and said unto his father, Bless me, even me also, O my father. And he said, THY BROTHER CAME WITH SUBTILTY, AND HATH TAKEN AWAY THY BLESSING. And he said, Is not he rightly named Jacob? for he hath supplanted me these two times: he took away my birthright; and, behold, now he hath taken away my blessing. And he said, Hast thou not reserved a blessing for me? And Isaac answered and said unto Esau, BEHOLD, I HAVE MADE HIM THY LORD, AND ALL HIS BRETHREN HAVE I GIVEN TO

17

HIM FOR SERVANTS; AND WITH CORN AND WINE HAVE I SUSTAINED HIM: AND WHAT SHALL I DO NOW UNTO THEE, MY SON?

Genesis 27:34-37

We succeed in life by blessings. The success of Jacob's life was determined by the blessings he received from his father, Isaac. Isaac blessed Jacob. Isaac made the brethren of Jacob into servants for Jacob. Isaac made Jacob into a lord. Isaac sustained Jacob with corn and wine. How did he do all these things? By blessing Jacob! The success of Jacob's life was determined by the blessing spoken over him by his father.

2. YOU START OUT IN LIFE BY BLESSINGS.

So God created man in his own image, in the image of God created he him; male and female created he them. And God blessed them, and God said unto them, be fruitful, and multiply, and replenish the earth, and subdue it: and have dominion over the fish of the sea, and over the fowl of the air, and over every living thing that moveth upon the earth. And God said, Behold, I have given you every herb bearing seed, which is upon the face of all the earth, and every tree, in the which is the fruit of a tree yielding seed; to you it shall be for meat. And to every beast of the earth, and to every fowl of the air, and to every thing that creepeth upon the earth, wherein there is life, I have given every green herb for meat: and it was so.

Genesis 1:27-30

The first thing God did for man was to bless him because man's destiny depended on the blessing. God did not provide a school or a university for Adam. He started him out with a blessing. A blessing is what you need to begin your life! If you start your ministry without a blessing it will not go far. Many pastors are unable to thrive because they did not start out in ministry with a blessing. Some started their ministry by stealing other people's congregations. Others started out in ministry by destroying other people's churches. Stealing and destroying do not bring blessings. When you start out without a blessing you can only expect failure.

Some want to start out their marriage in a beautiful place. Some want to start their marriage on an island. Some want to get married in a garden. Some want to get married on a beach. As they start out their new life they want to impress the world with an amazing display of fashion, money and prestige. They do not think of starting out with a blessing. Their minds are on earthly things. They do not mind if an unbeliever officiates their marriage. Their minds are not on the reality of blessings and curses.

God wanted Adam and Eve to start out with a blessing. They began their walk together with God's blessings. Even those who started out with a blessing were destroyed by the devil. How much more those who do not start out with a blessing?!

3.   YOU PREVAIL IN LIFE BY BLESSINGS.

Joseph is a fruitful bough, even a fruitful bough by a well; whose branches run over the wall:

The archers have sorely grieved him, and shot at him, and hated him:

But his bow abode in strength, and the arms of his hands were made strong by the hands of the mighty God of Jacob; (from thence is the shepherd, the stone of Israel:)

Even by the God of thy father, who shall help thee; and by the Almighty, who shall bless thee with blessings of heaven above, blessings of the deep that lieth under, blessings of the breasts, and of the womb: THE BLESSINGS OF THY FATHER HAVE PREVAILED ABOVE THE BLESSINGS OF MY PROGENITORS UNTO THE UTMOST BOUND OF THE EVERLASTING HILLS: they shall be on the head of Joseph, and on the crown of the head of him that was separate from his brethren.

Genesis 49:22-26

Joseph was hated by many people! The archers shot at him. He was accused of being a tell-tale. He was thrown into a pit. He was sold as a slave. He was accused of attempting to rape his master's wife. He was thrown into prison. Things went from bad to worse. He was forgotten in the prison. When he interpreted a dream successfully, it still did not make a difference to his life.

Few people overcome such odds. To prevail means to prove superior in strength and power. Joseph prevailed! To prevail also means to continue to exist. How did he prevail? Joseph prevailed by the blessings that he received from his father. The blessings he received were prevailing blessings. The blessings prevailed on him even unto the bound of the everlasting hills. The prevailing blessings of God will cause you to exist when you should have been wiped out.

4. YOU ARE RECOGNIZED IN LIFE BY YOUR BLESSINGS.

Isaiah prophesied that you would be recognized. What would you be recognized for? Would you be recognized for your education or your other achievements in this life? Certainly not! The word of God promises that you will be recognized as the seed that the Lord has blessed.

And their seed shall be known among the Gentiles, and their offspring among the people: ALL THAT SEE THEM SHALL ACKNOWLEDGE THEM, THAT THEY ARE THE SEED WHICH THE LORD HATH BLESSED.

Isaiah 61:9

5. YOU ARE DISTINGUISHED FROM OTHERS BY BLESSINGS.

And Isaac answered and said unto Esau, Behold, I have made him thy lord, and all his brethren have I given to him for servants; and with corn and wine have I sustained him: and what shall I do now unto thee, my son? And Esau said unto his father, Hast thou but one blessing, my father? Bless me, even me also, O my father. And Esau lifted up

20

his voice, and wept. And Isaac his father answered and said unto him, Behold, thy dwelling shall be the fatness of the earth, and of the dew of heaven from above;

And by thy sword shalt thou live, and shalt serve thy brother; and it shall come to pass when thou shalt have the dominion, that thou shalt break his yoke from off thy neck.

AND ESAU HATED JACOB BECAUSE OF THE BLESSING WHEREWITH HIS FATHER BLESSED HIM: and Esau said in his heart, The days of mourning for my father are at hand; then will I slay my brother Jacob.

Genesis 27:37-41

Blessings distinguish you from your brethren. You will be distinguished from your colleagues, your family and your friends by the grade of blessings on your life. Jacob received the highest grade of blessing. Esau also received a blessing, only it was of a much lower grade.

Esau hated Jacob because of the low-grade blessing that he had received from his father. He knew that the grade of blessing he had received from his father would determine his rank and status in this life. Jacob had been totally distinguished from his brethren by the superior grade blessing he had received.

CHAPTER 4

Labour for a Blessing

You will have to expend energy if you want to lay hold on a blessing. All through the Bible, those who received blessings had to labour for them. Abraham was more than a hundred years old when he was called of the Lord and had to climb a mountain. At more than a hundred years old, he had to carry wood and sacrifice on a mountain in order to lay hold on his blessings. If you are not prepared to work hard for your blessing you are not going to receive it.

Instead of spending all that money and time trying to be rich, spend the same amount of money and time to do things that bring you a blessing. *Abraham was not trying to be rich. He was trying to be blessed.* Try to understand the difference because there is a big difference between trying to be blessed and trying to be rich. Sometimes, the effort to lay hold on a blessing may look like madness. But I tell you it is worth it! It is worth spending all your time and money on trying to be blessed than trying to be rich. Remember the secret: the blessing of the Lord makes rich (Proverbs 10:22). *Why aim for riches when you can aim for a blessing?*

Isaac was equally obedient to God. He was asked to stay in a particular country and sow in the land. That is exactly what he did! He sowed in the land. He started a huge farm and gave himself to farming just so he could please God. Isaac was not trying to be rich. He was trying to be blessed. Isaac was trying to obey God and he ended up going forward and becoming very great. *Neither Abraham nor Isaac had a vision to be rich. They had a vision to obey God and they ended up becoming rich.*

Jacob also had to kill a goat and grill it for his father in order to be blessed. He worked very hard because his mother told him to. He ended up being blessed by his father, Isaac. It is not the wealth that Jacob had but rather his father's blessing that has made Israel what it is today. Jacob's wealth consisting of a flock of goats disappeared long ago, but the blessing has not disappeared. It has persisted through the centuries.

Being a blessed man makes you rich. That is why you must labour to become a blessed man. How wonderful it is to be a blessed person. A blessed man will have blessed children. Wealth and riches will be in the house of a blessed person. A blessed man will be righteous forever.

There are many things that you can do to obtain a blessing. Instead of doing things to obtain riches, do things that lead to blessings. Spend time and money on things that are specifically mentioned as things that generate blessings. Indeed, there are also many things that generate curses. Why aim to be rich when you can aim to be blessed? The secret is clear: aim for blessings because the blessing of the Lord will make you rich any way.

Our fathers and ancestors have already done things that have brought curses on us. They lied, they stole, they cheated and curses are following entire families, tribes and nations. It is time to do things that will invoke blessings. All through the Bible, we learn about things that actively stir up blessings and cause blessings to come upon our lives. In this chapter, I have a list of things that are well-known to induce blessings. Begin to do all of them and blessings will follow you.

When blessings have operated in your life for some time, they begin to outweigh the curses that may be in operation. It is very easy to invoke a curse. There are curses everywhere. A curse is a frustration, a difficulty and a dark place to be in. Nothing works when a curse is in operation. One of the ways to neutralize curses is to invoke blessings. If you are blessed to be the head, the curse to be "the tail" will be neutralized. Through blessings you keep neutralizing curses that have come to you through your own sins and the sins of your parents. Labour for a blessing! Labour for a blessing! Labour not to be rich! Rather, labour for a blessing!

A blessed man is someone who has received blessings for so long that he has become a blessed person. The blessings in his life outweigh the active curses and the summation of his life is "blessed". He is a blessed man. The Bible has a list of people who were blessed people. Indeed, their lives were different from those who were not blessed persons.

You must labour to become a blessed person. There are two things you can be. You can either be a blessed man or a cursed man. It is better to be a blessed person. Blessed is the man that fears the Lord (Psalms 112:1). When you fear the Lord you become a blessed person. There are amazing blessings for people who are called "blessed". May you be a truly blessed person! May you live in such a way that all men will point to you and say, "You are blessed!"

1. Labour for a blessing by keeping His commandments.

Praise ye the Lord. BLESSED is the man that feareth the Lord, that delighteth greatly in his commandments. His seed shall be mighty upon earth: the generation of the upright shall be blessed. Wealth and riches shall be in his house: and his righteousness endureth for ever.

Psalms 112:1-3

Those who fear God and delight in His commandments become blessed men. Work hard to obey God's commandments to your life. Obeying the commandments of God must be your life's goal. To labour means to strive towards a goal and to work very hard for it. Work very hard to keep the commandments of God. Strive to fear God.

When you obey God, you will receive a blessing from the Lord! The rewards of this blessing are out of this world! Your children will be mighty! Your whole generation will be blessed! Wealth and riches will be in your house! Your righteousness will endure forever.

Compare the rewards of this blessing to the rewards of a few dollars. Why would you strive for a few dollars when you could strive for a blessing?

2. Labour for a blessing by paying your tithes.

Will a man rob God? Yet ye have robbed me. But ye say, wherein have we robbed thee? In tithes and offerings! Ye are cursed with a curse: for ye have robbed me, even this whole nation. Bring ye all the tithes into the storehouse, that there may be meat in mine house, and prove me now herewith, saith the Lord of hosts, if I will not open you the windows of heaven, and pour you out a blessing, that there shall not be room enough to receive it. And I will rebuke the devourer for your sakes, and he shall not destroy the fruits of your ground; neither shall your vine cast her fruit before the time in the field, saith the Lord of hosts. AND ALL NATIONS SHALL CALL YOU BLESSED: FOR YE SHALL BE A DELIGHTSOME LAND, SAITH THE LORD OF HOSTS.

Malachi 3:8-12

Compare the earning of a few thousand dollars to getting the blessings of a tither. The blessings of a tither are out of this world. A tither is blessed to have the windows of heaven opened over his life. Above all, a tither has the devourers rebuked for his sake. The real causes of poverty are the devourers. Many Christians earn a lot of money but give it all away to the devourers. Paying rent, paying electricity bills, phone bills, garbage bills, property taxes, income taxes, school fees, water bills, mortgage, car repairs, car maintenance, purchasing clothes, hair extensions and food are all examples of devourers. With so many "mouths" wide open there is very little left over. God's blessing is far superior to any amount of money you could ever earn. Indeed, God's blessing is worth far more!

Labour to become a blessed person by paying your tithes. Tithe payers become blessed people. Labour for the blessings of those who pay tithes!

3. Labour for a blessing by serving God.

And YE SHALL SERVE THE LORD YOUR GOD, AND HE SHALL BLESS thy bread, and thy water; and I will take sickness away from the midst of thee. There shall nothing cast their young, nor be barren, in thy land: the number of thy days I will fulfil.

Exodus 23:25-26

If they obey and serve him, they shall spend their days in prosperity, and their years in pleasures.

Job 36:11

Your words have been stout against me, saith the Lord. Yet ye say, what have we spoken so much against thee? YE HAVE SAID, IT IS VAIN TO SERVE GOD: and what profit is it that we have kept his ordinance, and that we have walked mournfully before the Lord of hosts? And now we call the proud happy; yea, they that work wickedness are set up; yea, they that tempt God are even delivered. Then they that feared the Lord spake often one to another: and the Lord hearkened, and heard it , and a book of remembrance was written before him for them that feared the Lord , and that thought upon his name. And they shall be mine, saith the Lord of hosts, in that day when I make up my jewels; and I will spare them, as a man spareth his own son that serveth him. Then shall ye return, and discern between the righteous and the wicked, between him that serveth God and him that serveth him not.

Malachi 3:13-18

Labour to become a blessed person by serving God. There is a great blessing for those who serve God. Choosing to serve God is the greatest decision you could ever make. When you serve God, you labour and you work hard! But you are not labouring for money. You are not striving to pile up riches. You are striving to do the will of God. You want to serve God and experience His blessings.

Even when you earn money, it is not because you seek to pile up wealth. It is because you seek to do His will. Expect the blessings of those who serve God. He will bless your bread! He will bless your water! He will take sickness away from you! You will spend your days in pleasure and in prosperity!

4. Labour for a blessing by supporting the preaching of the gospel.

Now ye Philippians know also, that in the beginning of the gospel, when I departed from Macedonia, no church communicated with me as concerning giving and receiving, but ye only. For even in Thessalonica ye sent once and again unto my necessity. Not because I desire a gift: but I desire fruit that may abound to your account. But I have all, and abound: I am full, having received of Epaphroditus the things which were sent from you, an odour of a sweet smell, a sacrifice acceptable, wellpleasing to God. But my God shall supply all your need according to his riches in glory by Christ Jesus.

Philippians 4:15-19

Supporting the gospel is one of the ways to labour for a blessing. You cannot compare earning a few dollars with earning the blessing of those who support the gospel. What is the blessing of those who support the gospel? That blessing is simply God supplying all your needs according to His riches! Why labour for a few thousand dollars when you can labour for such a blessing?

We all have many diverse never-ending needs. It is our needs that drive us to work. We will never stop needing things. We will need things as long as we live. When you support the gospel, you can expect your needs to be taken care of for the rest of your life. Give yourself to working for the blessing that comes on those who support the gospel.

5. Labour for a blessing by remembering the poor.

When the Son of man shall come in his glory, and all the holy angels with him, then shall he sit upon the throne of his glory: And before him shall be gathered all nations: and he shall separate them one from another, as a shepherd divideth his sheep from the goats: And he shall set the sheep on his right hand, but the goats on the left. Then shall the King say unto them on his right hand, COME, YE BLESSED OF MY FATHER, inherit the kingdom prepared for you from the foundation of the world: For I was an hungred, and ye gave me meat: I was thirsty, and ye gave me drink: I was a stranger, and ye took me in: Naked, and ye clothed me: I was sick, and ye visited me: I was in prison, and ye came unto me. Then shall the righteous answer him, saying, Lord, when saw we thee an hungred, and fed thee? Or thirsty, and gave thee drink? When saw we thee a stranger, and took thee in? or naked, and clothed thee? Or when saw we thee sick, or in prison, and came unto thee? And the King shall answer and say unto them, Verily I say unto you, Inasmuch as ye have done it unto one of the least of these my brethren, ye have done it unto me.

Matthew 25:31-40

Remembering people who are in difficulty brings the blessing of God. Human beings will be divided into two groups: those who are blessed and those who are cursed. Those who are blessed are those who remembered the naked, the sick, the hungry, the thirsty and the strangers. A unique and special blessing worth far more than money comes on those who care for such people.

Labour to be blessed! Strive and work hard to be among those who care for people in difficulty. Your participation in such a ministry will only give rise to many blessings. A blessing is far more valuable than money. Labour to be blessed rather than labouring to be rich.

6. Labour for a blessing by sowing seeds.

Every man according as he purposeth in his heart, so let him give; not grudgingly, or of necessity: for God loveth a cheerful giver. And God is able to make all grace abound toward you; that ye, always having all sufficiency in all things, may abound to every good work: (As it is written, He hath dispersed abroad; he hath given to the poor: his righteousness remaineth for ever. Now he that ministereth seed to the sower both minister bread for your food, and multiply your seed sown, and increase the fruits of your righteousness;) Being enriched in every thing to all bountifulness, which causeth through us thanksgiving to God.

2 Corinthians 9:7-11

7. Labour for a blessing by honouring your prophet.

Let him that is taught in the word communicate unto him that teacheth in all good things. Be not deceived; God is not mocked: for whatsoever a man soweth, that shall he also reap. For he that soweth to his flesh shall of the flesh reap corruption; but he that soweth to the Spirit shall of the Spirit reap life everlasting. And let us not be weary in well doing: for in due season we shall reap, if we faint not. As we have therefore opportunity, let us do good unto all men, especially unto them who are of the household of faith.

Galatians 6:6-10

And she said unto her husband, Behold now, I perceive that this is an holy man of God, which passeth by us continually. Let us make a little chamber, I pray thee, on the wall; and let us set for him there a bed, and a table, and a stool, and a candlestick: and it shall be, when he cometh to us, that he shall turn in thither. And it fell on a day, that he came thither, and he turned into the chamber, and lay there. And he said to Gehazi his servant, call this Shunammite. And when he had called her, she stood before him. And he said unto him, Say now unto her, BEHOLD, THOU HAST BEEN CAREFUL FOR US WITH ALL THIS CARE; WHAT IS TO BE DONE FOR THEE? wouldest thou be spoken for to the king, or to the captain of the host? And she answered, I dwell among mine own people. And he said, What then is to be done for her? And Gehazi answered, Verily she hath no child, and her husband is old.

2 Kings 4:9-14

The Shunammite woman laboured to honour God's prophet. She built a home for him! She furnished his room with a bed, table and chair. She cared for him each time he passed through town. She served him for many years. One day, the prophet asked, WHAT IS TO BE DONE FOR THEE?" That is the only question that will be asked after you have honoured God's servant. "What is to be done for thee?"

Blessings abound for those who honour God's precious servants. The Shunammite woman received a child from the Lord. The blessing of receiving a child was greater than anything money could ever buy. She could have had all the money in the world but would never have had a child.

This Shunammite woman was wise in that she did not labour to be rich. She laboured to be blessed! Indeed, the blessing she received was worth far more than any money she would have earned in a lifetime. Today, the Shunammite woman's story encourages many people to labour for a blessing instead of labouring for money.

8. Labour for a blessing from the priests and pastors.

And Melchizedek king of Salem brought forth bread and wine: and he was the priest of the most high God. And he blessed him, and said, Blessed be Abram of the most high

30

God, possessor of heaven and earth: And blessed be the most high God, which hath delivered thine enemies into thy hand. And he gave him tithes of all.

Genesis 14:18-20

And the Lord spake unto Moses, saying, SPEAK UNTO AARON AND UNTO HIS SONS, SAYING, ON THIS WISE YE SHALL BLESS THE CHILDREN OF ISRAEL, SAYING UNTO THEM, THE LORD BLESS THEE, AND KEEP THEE: THE LORD MAKE HIS FACE SHINE UPON THEE, AND BE GRACIOUS UNTO THEE: The Lord lift up his countenance upon thee, and give thee peace. And they shall put my name upon the children of Israel; and I will bless them.

Numbers 6:22-27

The priests of God have a blessing to minister to God's people. God spoke to Moses saying "Teach Aaron how priests should bless the people." Priests are supposed to bless God's people. These blessings spoken by the priests will make a difference in your life. If these blessings would not make a difference, why would the priests be told to declare these blessings?

Labour for a blessing to be spoken over your life by the priest! It is a blessing for you when your pastor declares powerful words over your life. Do not take these words for granted. You will wage a good warfare through these words of prophecy.

9. Labour for a blessing in your prayer time.

AND JACOB WAS LEFT ALONE; and there wrestled a man with him until the breaking of the day. And when he saw that he prevailed not against him, he touched the hollow of his thigh; and the hollow of Jacob's thigh was out of joint, as he wrestled with him. And he said, let me go, for the day breaketh. AND HE SAID, I WILL NOT LET THEE GO, EXCEPT THOU BLESS ME. And he said unto him, what is thy name? And he said, Jacob. And he said, Thy name shall be called no more Jacob, but

31

Israel: for as a prince hast thou power with God and with men, and hast prevailed.

Genesis 32:24-28

Jacob did not labour to be rich. He laboured to be blessed! He struggled with an angel till the break of day. He would not let the angel go until the angel broke his leg with a swift karate strike. All that Jacob wanted was to be blessed! Jacob prayed all night because he wanted a blessing. He would not end the prayer meeting until he sensed the blessing of God.

Today, most people just desire to be rich. They fight, they struggle and they sacrifice everything for money. God's word teaches us not to do that. God's word teaches us that we should labour for blessings rather than labouring for riches. Every time you see something that brings about a blessing, remember that it is something you can and should labour for.

CHAPTER 5

Labour for the Blessings of Those Who Give

Give, and it shall be given unto you; good measure, pressed down, and shaken together, and running over, shall men give into your bosom. For with the same measure that ye mete withal it shall be measured to you again.

Luke 6:38

Instead of labouring to be rich, you must labour for the blessing that comes by giving. Instead of striving for wealth, strive for the blessing that comes from giving. Why work with all your heart to get rich, when you can work with all your heart for a blessing. Strive to enter the blessings that come on those who give.

Labour to give rather than labouring to be rich! Labouring to give is completely different from labouring to be rich. Labouring to give is to work very hard so that you can give money to support things that God touches your heart about. What a blessed life you have when you are labouring to give! No one can say that you are working aimlessly when you are labouring to give. No one can say that you are accumulating riches for nothing when you are labouring to give. Indeed, that is not the case. You are labouring to give!

Giving is the great spiritual key to prosperity. Instead of labouring to be rich, labour to be a giver.

I once saw a businessman working so hard. I could not understand what his aim was. He just wanted to bring certain machines into the country and sell them. He had no spiritual goals. He just wanted to acquire more and more money.

As I pondered over this businessman's life, I wished he had had some spiritual goals. But he simply wanted to have more and more money. I am sad to say that the harder he worked, the more he sunk into debt and confusion.

There are many businessmen like that today. They are labouring for nothing but to add to what they already have. They do not have an understanding of why they are alive or why they even work.

If you had as your goal, a desire to give certain amounts of money, it would bring meaning into your life. You would be labouring to give! Instead of doing meaningless work and piling up heaps of money that you can never use, you would have a good reason to live. Without a good reason for living and labouring, you will soon become depressed. Life is meaningless without having a good vision for your life. Labour not to be rich. This is what the word of God teaches. If you should not labour to be rich, what should you do? Answer is, "Labour to give!"

> **Therefore, as ye abound in every thing, in faith, and utterance, and knowledge, and in all diligence, and in your love to us, SEE THAT YE ABOUND IN THIS GRACE ALSO.**
>
> **2 Corinthians 8:7**

It is important to abound in your labour of giving. Many Christians do not abound in the grace of giving. They simply do not have the grace to give generously and repeatedly. Many people abound in the grace of showing off! Many people abound in the grace of caring for themselves but not so many people abound in the grace of giving. How do you abound in the grace of giving? You will abound in the grace of giving by learning how to give according to biblical standards.

1. Labour to be a giver who is also righteous and spiritual:

> And he shall sit as a refiner and purifier of silver: and he shall purify the sons of Levi, and purge them as gold and silver, THAT THEY MAY OFFER UNTO THE LORD AN OFFERING IN RIGHTEOUSNESS. Then shall the offering of Judah and Jerusalem be pleasant unto the Lord, as in the days of old, and as in former years.
>
> Malachi 3:3-4

You can give an offering to God in righteousness. There are many who are givers but are not spiritual. Many givers are thieves and therefore still have curses working robustly in their lives. Labour to be a person who is a giver and who is also spiritual.

There are many givers who are not spiritual. Labour to give in righteousness.

2. Labour to give out of your love for God.

Hereby perceive we the love of God, because he laid down his life for us: and we ought to lay down our lives for the brethren. But whoso hath this world's good, and seeth his brother have need, and shutteth up his bowels of compassion from him, how dwelleth the love of God in him?

1 John 3:16-17

Love is perceived through giving. You cannot say you love God without giving. Love is the basis for giving. God so loved the world that He gave His only begotten Son. Proper giving is the type that is done out of love. Unfortunately, many people do not give out of love. Some people give to make a show. Some people give because they have disposable cash. Why do you give? Labour to become someone who is driven by love for God.

3. Labour to give out of your respect for God.

A son honoureth his father, and a servant his master: if then I be a father, where is mine honour? and if I be a master, where is my fear? saith the Lord of hosts unto you, O priests, that despise my name. And ye say, wherein have we despised thy name? Ye offer polluted bread upon mine altar; and ye say, wherein have we polluted thee? In that ye say, the table of the Lord is contemptible. And if ye offer the blind for sacrifice, is it not evil? And if ye offer the lame and sick, is it not evil? Offer it now unto thy governor; will he be pleased with thee, or accept thy person? saith the Lord of hosts.

Malachi 1:6-8

Honour the Lord with thy substance, and with the firstfruits of all thine increase: So shall thy barns be filled with plenty, and thy presses shall burst out with new wine.

Proverbs 3:9-10

Labour to become someone who gives out of respect for God. There are those who give their polluted bread to God. There are those who give the lame and the blind to God. These gifts are negative because they rather show your lack of respect for God. Some gifts minister negativity rather than ministering blessings.

Be careful with what you present to God! Labour to give out of your respect for God. Labour to give out of your desire to honour God. If you honour God, you will honour His servants and you will honour those who speak for Him.

4. Labour to give according to your level of prosperity.

For if there be first a willing mind, it is accepted according to that a man hath, and not according to that he hath not.

2 Corinthians 8:12

The scripture is clear. You must give according to what you have! Your gift is accepted according to what you have. Most people do not give according to their level of prosperity. As you labour to give, you must grow in giving until you give according to your level of prosperity. As people prosper, they tend to give less and less. You would have thought that people would give more and more as they prosper. Giving is relative to what you have.

There are people who have a million dollars but would only give a hundred dollars to help evangelism. There are people who have three hundred dollars but give a hundred dollars away. The one who had three hundred dollars and gave a hundred dollars would have given over thirty per cent of his wealth away. The one who had a million dollars and gave a hundred dollars would have given only 0.01 per cent of his wealth away.

Indeed, most rich people do not give according to their prosperity. As they prosper, they feel that God deserves less and less of their wealth. Labour to give according to your wealth. Labour to give in such a way that is acceptable.

5. Labour to give cheerfully: happily and joyously. Otherwise don't give.

Every man according as he purposeth in his heart, so let him give; not grudgingly, or of necessity: for God loveth a cheerful giver.

2 Corinthians 9:7

You must labour to give cheerfully! God loves a cheerful giver and so do you! There are many times I have turned away from unwilling givers. You do not want to receive anything from the hand of a person who is unhappy to give. When a person is not giving something cheerfully, you even wonder if he is giving you a curse.

6. Labour to give sacrificially.

That ye be not slothful, but followers of them who through faith and patience inherit the promises.

Hebrews 6:12

Instead of labouring to be rich, you must labour to make sacrifices to God.

Making sacrifices to God is key to receiving blessings from God. You must labour to follow the sacrifices of those who have become famous for the amazing blessings they received because of their sacrifices. People have sacrificed a lot to God. It is time for you to follow that sacrifice.

The scripture is clear that we must follow people who are blessed; people who have inherited the promises of God.

To follow such people means to learn from them and walk in their sacrificial ways. Some of the blessed people we know about are Abraham who was very rich, David who was a man after God's heart and Solomon who was the wisest man on earth. All the characters mentioned have set an example of sacrifice for us to follow. Abraham set the example of making the ultimate sacrifice of his son. David set the example of loving God and loving His house. Solomon set the example of obeying his father and carrying out his father's wishes. Job set the example of surviving the most terrible tragedies and coming out shining with far more than he had before. Isaac set the example of staying in a country that was not doing well economically and still ending up being blessed.

Joseph of Arimathaea risked his life to show love to the body of Jesus Christ. That was a big sacrifice for someone who did not need to do that. Because of this, Joseph of Arimathaea is mentioned in every Bible all over the world, over two thousand years after Jesus died on the cross. His acts of sacrifice and loyalty have won him a place in the Bible for all time.

Zacchaeus of all people has also won a place in the Bible by completely repenting and turning away from his past life. Many Christians do not repent and fully turn away from their sins. Zacchaeus turned around and sacrificed half of his wealth for the kingdom of God.

CHAPTER 6

Labour for the Blessings of Church Builders

And it came to pass, when the king sat in his house, and the Lord had given him rest round about from all his enemies; That the king said unto Nathan the prophet, See now, I dwell in an house of cedar, but the ark of God dwelleth within curtains. And Nathan said to the king, Go, do all that is in thine heart; for the Lord is with thee.

And it came to pass that night, that the word of the Lord came unto Nathan, saying, GO AND TELL MY SERVANT DAVID, THUS SAITH THE LORD, SHALT THOU BUILD ME AN HOUSE FOR ME TO DWELL IN? Whereas I have not dwelt in any house since the time that I brought up the children of Israel out of Egypt, even to this day, but have walked in a tent and in a tabernacle.

In all the places wherein I have walked with all the children of Israel spake I a word with any of the tribes of Israel, whom I commanded to feed my people Israel, saying, Why build ye not me an house of cedar? NOW THEREFORE SO SHALT THOU SAY UNTO MY SERVANT DAVID, THUS SAITH THE LORD OF HOSTS, I took thee from the sheepcote, from following the sheep, to be ruler over my people, over

Israel: And I was with thee whithersoever thou wentest, and have cut off all thine enemies out of thy sight, and have made thee a great name, like unto the name of the great men that are in the earth. Moreover I will appoint a place for my people Israel, and will plant them, that they may dwell in a place of their own, and move no more; neither shall the children of wickedness afflict them any more, as beforetime, And as since the time that I commanded judges to be over my people Israel, and have caused thee to rest from all thine enemies. ALSO THE LORD TELLETH THEE THAT HE WILL MAKE THEE AN HOUSE.

And when thy days be fulfilled, and thou shalt sleep with thy fathers, I will set up thy seed after thee, which shall proceed out of thy bowels, and I will establish his kingdom.

2 Samuel 7:1-12

1. Labour to build the house of God and God will build a house for you!

When you build a house for God, God will build a house for you! Look at the scripture above. David attempted to build a house for God. God's response to David was that He would build a house for David. *"The Lord telleth thee that He will make thee an house."*

If you build a house for God, God will build a house for you! Building God's church brings tremendous favour into your life.

Instead of labouring to be rich, you must labour to build the church. Building a church will bring tremendous blessing into your life. Instead of striving to build your own house, strive to build the house of God. You are working with all your heart to get more money. Today, you can work with all your heart to build the house of God. It is time to have a good vision for your life.

Thou shalt arise, and have mercy upon Zion: for the time to favour her, yea, the set time, is come. For thy servants take pleasure in her stones, and favour the dust thereof.

Psalms 102:13-14

The time to favour God's people has come because they are interested in the stones and the dust of God's house. When God's people take an interest in His house, He favours them greatly.

2. Labour for the blessings of those who build the house of God.

Is it time for you, O ye, to dwell in your cieled houses, and this house lie waste? Now therefore thus saith the Lord of hosts; consider your ways. Ye have sown much, and bring in little; ye eat, but ye have not enough; ye drink, but ye are not filled with drink; ye clothe you, but there is none warm; and he that earneth wages earneth wages to put it into a bag with holes. Thus saith the Lord of hosts; Consider your ways. GO UP TO THE MOUNTAIN, AND BRING WOOD, AND BUILD THE HOUSE;

AND I WILL TAKE PLEASURE IN IT, AND I WILL BE GLORIFIED, SAITH THE LORD. YE LOOKED FOR MUCH, AND, LO, IT CAME TO LITTLE; AND WHEN YE BROUGHT IT HOME, I DID BLOW UPON IT. Why? saith the Lord of hosts. Because of mine house that is waste, and ye run every man unto his own house. Therefore the heaven over you is stayed from dew, and the earth is stayed from her fruit. And I called for a drought upon the land, and upon the mountains, and upon the corn, and upon the new wine, and upon the oil, and upon that which the ground bringeth forth, and upon men, and upon cattle, and upon all the labour of the hands.

Haggai 1:4-11

Why would you want God to blow on your salary? Why would you want God to blow your salary away? Instead of labouring to have a higher salary, labour to build the house of God so that God does not blow on your salary. God wants to bless you but He wants you to think about His house. Why do you not rise up and go to the mountain and cut some wood to build the house of God? The heavens over your head will open. The ground will bring forth her fruit.

3. **Labour to have a heart to build a house in the name of the Lord.**

And IT WAS IN THE HEART OF DAVID MY FATHER TO BUILD AN HOUSE FOR THE NAME OF THE LORD God of Israel. And the Lord said unto David my father, whereas it was in thine heart to build an house unto my name, THOU DIDST WELL THAT IT WAS IN THINE HEART. Nevertheless thou shalt not build the house; but thy son that shall come forth out of thy loins, he shall build the house unto my name.

1 Kings 8:17-19

When you have a heart to build the house of God, you do well. "Thou didst well that it was in thine heart." God is happy

43

that you are thinking about His house. God is impressed that you are thinking about His work. Labour to be like David. Labour to have the kind of heart he had! King David never laboured to be rich. Yet he died full of riches! Is it not interesting? Those who labour for riches often die without these riches. Those who do not labour for these riches are often given so much.

And he died in a good old age, FULL OF DAYS, RICHES, AND HONOUR: and Solomon his son reigned in his stead.

1 Chronicles 29:28

4. **Labour to gather money for the building of the house of God.**

Furthermore David the king said unto all the congregation, Solomon my son, whom alone God hath chosen, is yet young and tender, and the work is great: for the palace is not for man, but for the Lord God. NOW I HAVE PREPARED WITH ALL MY MIGHT FOR THE HOUSE OF MY GOD THE GOLD FOR THINGS TO BE MADE OF GOLD, and the silver for things of silver, and the brass for things of brass, the iron for things of iron, and wood for things of wood; onyx stones, and stones to be set, glistering stones, and of divers colours, and all manner of precious stones, and marble stones in abundance. Moreover, because I have set my affection to the house of my God, I have of mine own proper good, of gold and silver, which I have given to the house of my God, over and above all that I have prepared for the holy house,

1 Chronicles 29:1-3

Labour for the church to be built even if you do not get the glory for it! Have a heart to raise money to build the house of God. Stick your neck out and take some embarrassment for the house of God. Fight for the church to have land! Fight for the church to have property! It is not only pastors who must build churches. All those who love God must build His house. Look at how King David ended: full of days, full of riches and full of honour! King David never laboured for riches. And yet he died full of riches.

5.   Labour to build the cities of God.

Cry yet, saying, thus saith the Lord of hosts; MY CITIES THROUGH PROSPERITY SHALL YET BE SPREAD ABROAD; and the Lord shall yet comfort Zion, and shall yet choose Jerusalem.

Zechariah 1:17

The cities of God are a series of church buildings. Through your prosperity, let the cities of God be spread abroad. The cities of God speak of the many buildings that must be built in the name of God during our lifetime. When we put together all the churches you have built, it will form a veritable city. Labour to build the cities of God!

CHAPTER 7

Labour to Become a Blessing

Instead of labouring to be rich, you must labour to become a blessing to others. Instead of striving for wealth, strive to become a blessing. Why work with all your heart to get money, when you can work with all your heart to help others. It is time for you to decide to become a blessing to many people. It is far greater to become a blessing than just to be a blessed person!

Your ultimate vision for life must be to labour to be a blessing. Beyond a certain amount of income there is no benefit to the receiver. Beyond a certain number of houses you can no longer safely control what you have.

I would like to be like Abraham who became a blessing to the whole world. God said to Abraham, "All nations will be blessed through you"(Genesis 12:3). This is how God called Abraham. He called Abraham to bless him so that he would be a blessing to the nations of the world. *You never find Abraham labouring to be rich. You find him labouring to obey God.* You find him labouring to please his Creator. Yet you find him becoming a blessing to the whole of mankind. Those who labour to be rich never achieve the heights that Abraham achieved.

Paul warned all Christians and declared that rich people should be rich in good works. They should be seen as givers. They should be seen to be doing good things and distributing their wealth. He said that this would create a good foundation for them in eternity.

Notice Hannah's vision. All she wanted was to have a child that she could give away. She did not want a child that she could keep. She did not want a child that she could play with and enjoy like any other mother. Because she was labouring to be a blessing, God opened her womb and gave her that child and much more.

It is rare to see people have a life's goal of building God's house. Most people's life's goals have to do with establishing their own houses and increasing their personal wealth. In this chapter, you will see people whose goals were to be a blessing to others. It was not about themselves. It was all about God and His kingdom.

Be a blessing to others! This is the highest call! The call to be a blessing! God is calling you today to be a blessing to many people. Some people are blessed but they never become a blessing to others. You must rise up to the challenge and become a blessing to others.

1. **Labour to be a blessing to the whole world like Abraham was a blessing to the whole world.** Abraham never tried to be a rich man. He never laboured to be rich. Today, he stands out as the man who became a blessing to the whole world. How did he become a blessing to the whole world? By labouring to obey God no matter what.

    Now the Lord had said unto Abram, Get thee out of thy country, and from thy kindred, and from thy father's house, unto a land that I will shew thee: And I will make of thee a great nation, and I will bless thee, and make thy name great; and THOU SHALT BE A BLESSING: And I will bless them that bless thee, and curse him that curseth thee: and in thee shall all families of the earth be blessed.

    Genesis 12:1-3

47

2. **Labour to be a blessing to many people according to the instructions of Paul.** Paul's instructions are clear. Have good works! Do good things! Don't be high-minded! Help other people! Labour to be a blessing!

CHARGE THEM THAT ARE RICH in this world, that they be not highminded, nor trust in uncertain riches, but in the living God, who giveth us richly all things to enjoy; THAT THEY DO GOOD, THAT THEY BE RICH IN GOOD WORKS, ready to distribute, willing to communicate; Laying up in store for themselves a good foundation against the time to come, that they may lay hold on eternal life. O Timothy, keep that which is committed to thy trust, avoiding profane and vain babblings, and oppositions of science falsely so called: Which some professing have erred concerning the faith. Grace be with thee. Amen.

1 Timothy 6:17-21

3. **Labour to be a blessing to the ministry like Hannah:** "Give me a child so I can give him away to become a prophet." She labored to be pregnant just so that she could give away the child. What an amazing testimony of laboring to be a blessing. How many people work so hard just so they can give everything away?

And she vowed a vow, and said, O Lord of hosts, if thou wilt indeed look on the affliction of thine handmaid, and remember me, and not forget thine handmaid, but wilt give unto thine handmaid a man child, THEN I WILL GIVE HIM UNTO THE LORD all the days of his life, and there shall no razor come upon his head.

1 Samuel 1:11

4. **Labour to be a blessing to others in the kingdom of God.** Seeking the kingdom of God first is seeking to be a blessing. Instead of seeking your personal wealth, you seek the wealth of God's kingdom. As you seek the interests of God's kingdom, you will end up having all things.

(For after all these things do the Gentiles seek:) for your heavenly Father knoweth that ye have need of all these things. But seek ye first the kingdom of god, and his righteousness; and all these things shall be added unto you.

Matthew 6:32-33

CHAPTER 8

Labour for Supernatural Provision

But my GOD SHALL SUPPLY all your need according to his riches in glory by Christ Jesus.

Philippians 4:19

My God shall supply! God supplies provisions! God sends supernatural supplies! God is a supplier! God gives supernatural provisions! God can send supernatural supplies to you! My God shall supply! God is the source of all supernatural supplies.

What is a supernatural supply? It is a mystical supply of whatever you need. Supernatural supply is the use of divine power to meet your needs. This mystical supply from God takes place through extraordinary and paranormal methods. In the natural, such provision could never take place. *Jesus Christ feeding five thousand people with five loaves and two fish is an example of this paranormal, mystical supply.*

Instead of labouring to be rich, labour for the blessing of supernatural and mystical supplies. Instead of striving for riches, strive to receive the blessing of paranormal and mystical supplies from heaven. Why work with all your heart to get money, when you can work with all your heart to have a blessing?

The blessing of having a supernatural supply of money is a real thing. Money and supplies do not only come from hard work. Salaried workers find it hard to believe that there is a supernatural way of receiving an income.

It is important that Christians believe in the supernatural part of God's word. You cannot only believe in things that are logical. Many things in the Old and New Testament are supernatural. You are either going to be a believer in these things or a doubter. God has stated clearly, "…It is He that giveth thee power to get wealth…" (Deuteronomy 8:18). It means that there is a "Power to get wealth". Notice the scripture below; His divine power gives us all things.

According as HIS DIVINE POWER HATH GIVEN UNTO US ALL THINGS that pertain unto life and godliness, through the knowledge of him that hath called us to glory and virtue:

2 Peter 1:3

His divine power gives us all things that pertain to this life and godliness. Once you believe in the invisible power of God, you are opening yourself up to receiving a supernatural supply of finances. Expect divine power to bring you mystical and heavenly supplies.

Just as people believe in the supernatural ability of God to heal disease and sickness, you must open yourself up to believe in the supernatural supply of money. God shall supply! God will supply! There are several examples of supernatural, mystical, paranormal provision that came through pure divine power. This is what you must labour for. Labour for supernatural provision. Expect God to intervene! See what he did for others and expect Him to do it for you.

1. Labour for supernatural supplies for your mission.

And he called unto him the twelve, and began to send them forth by two and two; and gave them power over unclean spirits; And commanded them that they should TAKE NOTHING FOR THEIR JOURNEY, SAVE A STAFF ONLY; NO SCRIP, NO BREAD, NO MONEY IN THEIR PURSE: But be shod with sandals; and not put on two coats.

Mark 6:7-9

AND HE SAID UNTO THEM, WHEN I SENT YOU WITHOUT PURSE, AND SCRIP, AND SHOES, LACKED YE ANY THING? AND THEY SAID, NOTHING. Then said he unto them, But now, he that hath a purse, let him take it, and likewise his scrip: and he that hath no sword, let him sell his garment, and buy one.

Luke 22:35-36

Jesus sent His disciples on a mission without money. His instructions were clear. Do not take any money, do not take a bag, do not take any food. Can you imagine being sent on a journey from London to Zambia without any money, food or bags? How are you expected to buy your ticket? How are you expected to survive? How are you expected to eat? How are you expected to pay for your accommodation? Indeed, it even sounds absurd to think that someone could be sent on a journey under such conditions.

But it is not absurd if you believe in the supernatural and mystical supply of God. God will send you everything that you need. God will provide the money you need for your church. God will provide the money you need for your mission. God will provide you with cars, fuel and accommodation. God will give you everything you need. Men of little faith always reject the possibility and reality of the divine provision of God. Expect God to take care of you through paranormal, mystical, unusual and extraordinary means.

2. Labour for supernatural supplies to fulfil your obligations.

He saith, Yes. And when he was come into the house, Jesus prevented him, saying, What thinkest thou, Simon? Of whom do the kings of the earth take custom or tribute? of their own children, or of strangers? Peter saith unto him, of strangers. Jesus saith unto him, then are the children free. Notwithstanding, lest we should offend them, GO THOU TO THE SEA, AND CAST AN HOOK, AND TAKE UP THE FISH THAT FIRST COMETH UP; AND WHEN THOU HAST OPENED HIS MOUTH, THOU SHALT FIND A PIECE OF MONEY: that take, and give unto them for me and thee.

Matthew 17:25-27

Jesus paid His tax with a supernatural supply. He sent His disciples fishing. He must have told Simon, "Go fishing and you will find a mystical, paranormal, supernatural fish which will have a coin in its mouth. This coin will be so valuable that you will be able to pay all our obligations. We will be able to pay all our bills and taxes."

I know that some religious people would wish that this scripture was not in the Bible. But it is! God can send money to you supernaturally. God can provide for you outside your job. God can send mystical supplies to take care of everything you need. It is time to wake up to this reality. Labour for supernatural supplies! Supernatural supplies are real!

3. Labour for supernatural supplies for thousands of people.

Jesus fed five thousand people with supernatural supplies. Most of us cannot take three or four people to the restaurant. Jesus took five thousand people to the restaurant and fed them until they were filled. Many times people are still hungry after eating. But these people were filled to the extent that they had to gather the remains of the food. As you grow in ministry, thousands of people will come to you for help. You will have to provide for the needs of many people. You may need to provide a sound system or a lighting system to cater for thousands of people. You may need to provide books for thousands of people. You may even need to provide food for thousands of people. Through the supernatural power of God, you will be able to take care of the needs of people. Angels will be sent from heaven to provide and to multiply everything in your hand.

When Jesus then lifted up his eyes, and saw a great company come unto him, he saith unto Philip, Whence shall we buy bread, that these may eat? And this he said to prove him: for he himself knew what he would do. Philip answered him, Two hundred pennyworth of bread is not sufficient for them, that every one of them may take a little. One of his disciples, Andrew, Simon Peter's brother, saith unto him, There is a lad here, which hath five barley loaves, and two small fishes: but what are they among so many? And Jesus said, Make the men sit down. Now there was much grass in the place.

SO THE MEN SAT DOWN, IN NUMBER ABOUT FIVE THOUSAND. And JESUS TOOK THE LOAVES; AND WHEN HE HAD GIVEN THANKS, HE DISTRIBUTED

TO THE DISCIPLES, AND THE DISCIPLES TO THEM
THAT WERE SET DOWN; AND LIKEWISE OF THE
FISHES AS MUCH AS THEY WOULD. When they were
filled, he said unto his disciples, Gather up the fragments
that remain, that nothing be lost.

John 6:5-12

4. Labour for supernatural supplies for your business.

And it came to pass, that, as the people pressed upon
him to hear the word of God, he stood by the lake of
Gennesaret, And saw two ships standing by the lake: but
the fishermen were gone out of them, and were washing
their nets. And he entered into one of the ships, which was
Simon's, and prayed him that he would thrust out a little
from the land. And he sat down, and taught the people
out of the ship. Now when he had left speaking, he said
unto Simon, Launch out into the deep, and let down your
nets for a draught. And Simon answering said unto him,
MASTER, WE HAVE TOILED ALL THE NIGHT, AND
HAVE TAKEN NOTHING: NEVERTHELESS AT THY
WORD I WILL LET DOWN THE NET. AND WHEN
THEY HAD THIS DONE, THEY INCLOSED A GREAT
MULTITUDE OF FISHES: AND THEIR NET BRAKE.
And they beckoned unto their partners, which were in the
other ship, that they should come and help them. And they
came, and filled both the ships, so that they began to sink.
When Simon Peter saw it, he fell down at Jesus' knees,
saying, Depart from me; for I am a sinful man, O Lord.

Luke 5:1-8

Jesus helped Peter's fishing business with a supernatural
supply. Once again, Jesus provided for His disciples miraculously.
They had toiled all night and caught nothing. Their own labour
had yielded nothing. At the command of Jesus their nets were
filled and began to break. Expect net-breaking, ship-sinking
provisions! This is nothing less than supernatural, extraordinary
and mystical provision. There is nothing normal about what
happened by the lake of Gennesaret. Peter's business was

transformed at the words of Jesus. Jesus was not a professional fisherman. His background was carpentry and he was a minister of the gospel. By the supernatural power of God, He gave the right command and riches, wealth and prosperity came in instantly. When you act on the word that comes from God's servant, you will prosper supernaturally.

5. Labour for supernatural supplies for your work.

After these things Jesus shewed himself again to the disciples at the sea of Tiberias; and on this wise shewed he himself. There were together Simon Peter, and Thomas called Didymus, and Nathanael of Cana in Galilee, and the sons of Zebedee, and two other of his disciples. Simon Peter saith unto them, I go a fishing. They say unto him, We also go with thee. They went forth, and entered into a ship immediately; and that night they caught nothing. But when the morning was now come, Jesus stood on the shore: but the disciples knew not that it was Jesus. Then JESUS SAITH UNTO THEM, CHILDREN, HAVE YE ANY MEAT? THEY ANSWERED HIM, NO. AND HE SAID UNTO THEM, CAST THE NET ON THE RIGHT SIDE OF THE SHIP, AND YE SHALL FIND. THEY CAST THEREFORE, AND NOW THEY WERE NOT ABLE TO DRAW IT FOR THE MULTITUDE OF FISHES. THEREFORE THAT DISCIPLE WHOM JESUS LOVED SAITH UNTO PETER, IT IS THE LORD. Now when Simon Peter heard that it was the Lord, he girt his fisher's coat unto him, (for he was naked,) and did cast himself into the sea. And the other disciples came in a little ship; (for they were not far from land, but as it were two hundred cubits,) dragging the net with fishes. As soon then as they were come to land, they saw a fire of coals there, and fish laid thereon, and bread. Jesus saith unto them, Bring of the fish which ye have now caught. Simon Peter went up, and drew the net to land full of great fishes, an hundred and fifty and three: and for all there were so many, yet was not the net broken.

John 21:1-11

Peter received supernatural supplies when he followed the instructions of Jesus. This miracle of over-abundant provision was so characteristic that John recognised it. He said to Peter, "It is the Lord." It is only the Lord who provides in this way! Truly, you will begin to recognize the supernatural provision of God in your life. You will know that only God can do certain things. Expect your work to be transformed into a place of miraculous supply!

6. Labour for supernatural supplies in the wilderness of your life.

And they took their journey from Elim, and all the congregation of the children of Israel came unto the wilderness of Sin, which is between Elim and Sinai, on the fifteenth day of the second month after their departing out of the land of Egypt. And the whole congregation of the children of Israel murmured against Moses and Aaron in the wilderness: And the children of Israel said unto them, Would to God we had died by the hand of the Lord in the land of Egypt, when we sat by the flesh pots, and when we did eat bread to the full; for ye have brought us forth into this wilderness, to kill this whole assembly with hunger.

Then said the Lord unto Moses, BEHOLD, I WILL RAIN BREAD FROM HEAVEN FOR YOU; AND THE PEOPLE SHALL GO OUT AND GATHER A CERTAIN RATE EVERY DAY, THAT I MAY PROVE THEM, WHETHER THEY WILL WALK IN MY LAW, OR NO.

Exodus 16:1-4

You will definitely have to go through a wilderness in your life. The children of Israel were fed supernaturally through the wilderness. As God led the Israelites through the wilderness, He provided for them. They were never thirsty and they were never hungry. He clave the rock and waters gushed out. He made water flow out of rocks.

He rained bread from heaven. These are all supernatural, mystical and paranormal methods of getting bread and meat. These stories are there to prove to us that there is a supernatural, supernormal, parahuman, mystical and divine way of receiving supplies from heaven. I need you to believe in the supernatural supply for God's people. Whatever God did for the Israelites, He will do for you! He is doing it for you!

And they thirsted not when he led them through the deserts: HE CAUSED THE WATERS TO FLOW OUT OF THE ROCK FOR THEM: he clave the rock also, and the waters gushed out.

Isaiah 48:21

7. Labour for supernatural supplies in the midst of a famine.

AND THERE WAS A GREAT FAMINE IN SAMARIA: and, behold, they besieged it, until an ass's head was sold for fourscore pieces of silver, and the fourth part of a cab of dove's dung for five pieces of silver. And as the king of Israel was passing by upon the wall, there cried a woman unto him, saying, Help, my lord, O king. And he said, If the Lord do not help thee, whence shall I help thee? out of the barnfloor, or out of the winepress?

And the king said unto her, what aileth thee? AND SHE ANSWERED, THIS WOMAN SAID UNTO ME, GIVE THY SON, THAT WE MAY EAT HIM TO DAY, AND WE WILL EAT MY SON TO MORROW. SO WE BOILED MY SON, AND DID EAT HIM: and I said unto her on the next day, Give thy son, that we may eat him: and she hath hid her son. And it came to pass, when the king heard the words of the woman, that he rent his clothes; and he passed by upon the wall, and the people looked, and, behold, he had sackcloth within upon his flesh. Then he said, God do so and more also to me, if the head of Elisha the son of Shaphat shall stand on him this day. But Elisha sat in his house, and the elders sat with him; and the king sent a man from before him: but ere the messenger came to him, he said to the elders, See ye how this son of a murderer hath sent to take away mine head? Look, when the messenger cometh, shut the door, and hold him fast at the door: is not the sound of his master's feet behind him?

2 Kings 6:25-32

THEN ELISHA SAID, HEAR YE THE WORD OF THE LORD; THUS SAITH THE LORD, TO MORROW ABOUT THIS TIME SHALL A MEASURE OF FINE FLOUR BE SOLD FOR A SHEKEL, AND TWO MEASURES OF BARLEY FOR A SHEKEL, IN THE GATE OF SAMARIA. Then a lord on whose hand the king leaned answered the man of God, and said, Behold, if the Lord would make windows in heaven, might this thing be? And he said, Behold, thou shalt see it with thine eyes, but shalt not eat thereof.

2 Kings 7:1-2

The famine of Samaria was ended by a supernatural supply through the ministry of Elisha. This famine was so extreme that people were eating their children. God brought a supernatural supply that ended the drought. Expect a supernatural supply to end the stalemate in your life. Notice that it took the supernatural intervention of a prophet to end the financial dry season. All dry seasons in your life are coming to an end now. Expect God to do great things in your life! The power of God is more than enough to wipe out every great famine in your life.

8. Labour for supernatural supplies by believing in the prophet.

And it came to pass after a while, that the brook dried up, because there had been no rain in the land. And the word of the Lord came unto him, saying, Arise, get thee to Zarephath, which belongeth to Zidon, and dwell there: behold, I have commanded a widow woman there to sustain thee. So he arose and went to Zarephath. And when he came to the gate of the city, behold, the widow woman was there gathering of sticks: and he called to her, and said, Fetch me, I pray thee, a little water in a vessel, that I may drink.

And as she was going to fetch it, he called to her, and said, Bring me, I pray thee, a morsel of bread in thine hand. And she said, As the Lord thy God liveth, I have not a cake, but an handful of meal in a barrel, and a little oil in a cruse: and, behold, I am gathering two sticks, that I may go in and dress it for me and my son, that we may eat it, and die.

And Elijah said unto her, Fear not; go and do as thou hast said: but make me thereof a little cake first, and bring it unto me, and after make for thee and for thy son. For thus saith the Lord God of Israel, THE BARREL OF MEAL SHALL NOT WASTE, NEITHER SHALL THE CRUSE OF OIL FAIL, UNTIL THE DAY THAT THE LORD SENDETH RAIN UPON THE EARTH. And she went and did according to the saying of Elijah: and she, and he, and her house, did eat many days.

1 Kings 17:7-15

The widow of Zarephath declared that she was about to die. "I am having my last meal and after that I am ready to die." Then came Elijah the prophet with miraculous, supernatural, superhuman, paranormal, mystical and divine provision. Through Elijah, this widow of Zarephath received financial provision. She was told very clearly that her oil would not run out until the rainy season began. Through this word, her life was saved. The widow of Zarephath was fed by supernatural and mystical supply through the ministry of Elijah.

9. Labour for supernatural supplies to end a life of debt.

Many people are in debt. Many people do not believe that they can live without debt. Debt is used by satan to trap many people. Many churches are trapped and restrained because of their debts. Many families are down and under because of their debts. Supernatural power and provision are available to cancel debt! Supernatural power and provision are available so that you can live a life without debt.

Just as it happened in the days of Elisha, many prophets, evangelists and teachers are in debt today. There were debts in those days and there are debts today. Believe in supernatural provision and you will live a life without debts. Most of the people I told not to have debts did not believe me. Unfortunately, many of them are trapped and snared in a life of debt today. Believe in supernatural provision. Believe that God can take care of you!

Now there cried a certain woman of the wives of the sons of the prophets unto Elisha, saying, Thy servant my husband is dead; and thou knowest that thy servant did fear the Lord: and the creditor is come to take unto him my two sons to be bondmen. And Elisha said unto her, what shall I do for thee? Tell me, what hast thou in the house? And she said, Thine handmaid hath not any thing in the house, save a pot of oil. Then he said, Go, borrow thee vessels abroad of all thy neighbours, even empty vessels; borrow not a few. And when thou art come in, thou shalt shut the door upon thee and upon thy sons, and shalt pour out into all those vessels, and thou shalt set aside that which is full. So she went from him, and shut the door upon her and upon her sons, who brought the vessels to her; and she poured out. And it came to pass, when the vessels were full, that she said unto her son, Bring me yet a vessel. And he said unto her, there is not a vessel more. And the oil stayed. Then she came and told the man of God. And he said, Go, sell the oil, and pay thy debt, and live thou and thy children of the rest.

2 Kings 4:1-7

10. Labour for supernatural supplies for your leadership.

Thus saith the Lord to his anointed, to Cyrus, whose right hand I have holden, to subdue nations before him; and I will loose the loins of kings, to open before him the two leaved gates; and the gates shall not be shut; I will go before thee, and make the crooked places straight: I will break in pieces the gates of brass, and cut in sunder the bars of iron: AND I WILL GIVE THEE THE TREASURES

OF DARKNESS, AND HIDDEN RICHES OF SECRET PLACES, THAT THOU MAYEST KNOW THAT I, THE LORD, WHICH CALL THEE BY THY NAME, AM THE GOD OF ISRAEL.

Isaiah 45:1-3

King Cyrus received a supernatural supply of riches. King Cyrus was anointed by God to receive supernatural provision. In this mystical supply, he would discover the treasures of darkness and the hidden riches of secret places. This is what is going to happen under your leadership. Through the anointing, you will discover hidden money. Treasures which people have hidden will be brought out and given to you. Do you believe in such things? Do you believe that it is just a good salary that you need? God can do greater things than your salary and your bonuses can. He can give to you the hidden riches of secret places.

11. Labour for supernatural supplies for your new life.

HE BROUGHT THEM FORTH ALSO WITH SILVER AND GOLD: and there was not one feeble person among their tribes. Egypt was glad when they departed: for the fear of them fell upon them. He spread a cloud for a covering; and fire to give light in the night. THE PEOPLE ASKED, AND HE BROUGHT QUAILS, AND SATISFIED THEM WITH THE BREAD OF HEAVEN. HE OPENED THE ROCK, AND THE WATERS GUSHED OUT; THEY RAN IN THE DRY PLACES LIKE A RIVER. For he remembered his holy promise, and Abraham his servant. And he brought forth his people with joy, and his chosen with gladness: AND GAVE THEM THE LANDS OF THE HEATHEN: AND THEY INHERITED THE LABOUR OF THE PEOPLE; that they might observe his statutes, and keep his laws. Praise ye the Lord.

Psalms 105:37-45

The Psalms summarise the supernatural, superhuman, paranormal, mystical and divine provision that the Jews experienced as they marched out of Egypt into the Promised Land.

The Jews who came out of Egypt left with a supernatural supply of silver and gold.

The Jews received supernatural bread from heaven.

The Jews received supernatural supply of chicken, called quails.

The Jews had a supernatural supply of fresh water in the desert.

The Jews inherited lands in The Promised Land.

For four hundred years, the Israelites were impoverished slaves. In twenty-four hours, God made them millionaires. They walked out of Egypt with the gold and treasures of the Egyptians. Through many miracles and supernatural interventions, the Egyptians were willing to give up their wealth to the Israelites. This is what is going to happen in your life and ministry.

Only God can make people willing and eager to give up their wealth. People are very tight-fisted and most do not want to give up their secret wealth. As you enter your season of supernatural provision, you will see people's attitude changing. Through the divine and mystical power of God, people will release into your care wealth that you have never imagined.

CHAPTER 9

Labour for the Supernatural Supply

BUT MY GOD SHALL SUPPLY all your need according to his riches in glory by Christ Jesus.

Philippians 4:19

My God shall supply! God supernaturally supplies provisions! God supernaturally sends supplies! God is a supernatural supplier! God gives supernatural provisions! God can send supernatural supplies to you! My God shall supernaturally supply! God is the source of all supernatural supplies.

1. Labour for supernatural provision by believing in the anointing for wealth.

Beware that thou forget not the Lord thy God, in not keeping his commandments, and his judgments, and his statutes, which I command thee this day: Lest when thou hast eaten and art full, and hast built goodly houses, and dwelt therein; And when thy herds and thy flocks multiply, and thy silver and thy gold is multiplied, and all that thou hast is multiplied; . . .

But thou shalt remember the Lord thy God: FOR IT IS HE THAT GIVETH THEE POWER TO GET WEALTH, that he may establish his covenant which he sware unto thy fathers, as it is this day.

Deuteronomy 8:11-13, 18

Do you believe in the anointing for wealth? There is such an anointing as the anointing for wealth. The anointing for wealth is a spiritual power that creates mystical wealth and supply. The anointing for wealth creates a supernatural supply of fullness, flocks, goodly houses, silver and gold. Believe in it and you will receive it.

2. Labour for supernatural provision by being godly.

For bodily exercise profiteth little: BUT GODLINESS IS PROFITABLE UNTO ALL THINGS, having promise of the life that now is, and of that which is to come. This is a faithful saying and worthy of all acceptation.

1 Timothy 4:8-9

Godliness affects all things including finances. There is a direct correlation between a godly life and financial provision from God. If you are a thief, a curse will operate in your life. You cannot steal and expect God's provision to work with you. Begin to practice godliness and you will see God's hand moving in your finances.

3. Labour for supernatural provision by believing in the grace for wealth.

And GOD IS ABLE TO MAKE ALL GRACE ABOUND TOWARD YOU; THAT YE, ALWAYS HAVING ALL SUFFICIENCY in all things, may abound to every good work: (As it is written, He hath dispersed abroad; he hath given to the poor: his righteousness remaineth for ever.

2 Corinthians 9:8-9

If you care to read the scripture above, you will see that God makes grace to abound so that you have sufficiency. Grace is a supernatural and spiritual force. By the grace of God you will come out of poverty. By the grace of God, all your needs will be met! God is able to make all grace abound towards you. Receive supernatural grace and walk in it! Do you need a car? Do you need a house? Do you need money? Grace will provide all these things for you.

4. Labour for supernatural provision by believing in giving and receiving.

Give, and it shall be given unto you; good measure, pressed down, and shaken together, and running over, shall men give into your bosom. For with the same measure that ye mete withal it shall be measured to you again.

Luke 6:38

Giving is the key that unlocks supernatural provision. Jesus taught us to give. He said that giving would release people to come to your life with provisions. Why would somebody come into your life with the car you need, the house you need or the money you need? Something has to prompt that person to give

66

to you. Something has to guide that person to you. Something has to make people give to you. Jesus said: every time you give, you invoke the mysterious power of God to cause people to bring mystical provisions to you. Believe in the word of God and you will see it happen practically.

5. Labour for supernatural provision by believing that God makes people rich and God makes people poor.

The Lord maketh poor, and maketh rich: he bringeth low, and lifteth up.

1 Samuel 2:7

According to this scripture, God can make you poor or He can make you rich.

God has the power to transform you into a rich person. I do not know exactly how He will do that. But I know that He does such things. God can also turn you into a poor person. He can take away your wealth and make you a poor man. I do not know how He will do that but there are many things that angels do.

6. Labour for supernatural provision by believing in hard work.

He becometh poor that dealeth with a slack hand: but the hand of the diligent maketh rich.

Proverbs 10:4

The word of God acknowledges the role of hard work in prosperity.

Hard work and diligence make a person rich. However, we all know people who work very hard but are still not rich. There are many hardworking salaried workers in the world.

Not many of these salaried workers prosper to a certain level in the world. You will need more than hard work if you are to enter certain realms of prosperity. You need the blessing of God! *The blessing of the Lord maketh rich!* The blessings of God will raise you up into high levels of prosperity.

CHAPTER 10

Labour for Revelation

Instead of labouring to be rich, you must labour for revelation. Instead of striving for wealth, strive for revelation. Why work with all your heart to get money, when you can work with all your heart to receive revelation from God?

Revelation is the great gift that God gives to His children. A revelation is a word from God. A revelation is light from heaven. This light will guide you into the very place that you need to be. The Holy Spirit will give you ideas, wisdom, knowledge, understanding and counsel. Revelation is what you need to seek for. Labour not to be rich! Labour for revelation of God's word! It is the revelation you have that will make you rich. All through the Bible you see the effect of revelation.

And said, If thou wilt diligently hearken to the voice of the Lord thy God, and wilt do that which is right in his sight, and wilt give ear to his commandments, and keep all his statutes, I will put none of these diseases upon thee, which I have brought upon the Egyptians: for I AM THE LORD THAT HEALETH THEE.

Exodus 15:26

Thus saith the Lord, thy Redeemer, the Holy One of Israel;
I AM THE LORD THY GOD WHICH TEACHETH
THEE TO PROFIT, which leadeth thee by the way that
thou shouldest go. O that thou hadst hearkened to my
commandments! then had thy peace been as a river, and
thy righteousness as the waves of the sea: Thy seed also
had been as the sand, and the offspring of thy bowels like
the gravel thereof; his name should not have been cut off
nor destroyed from before me.

Isaiah 48:17-19

In the Bible, God introduces Himself to us in different ways.
I have reproduced two different scriptures that introduce God in
two different ways.

In Exodus, God introduces Himself as the One who heals.
In Isaiah He introduces Himself as the One who teaches you to
profit. To profit means "to ascend", to "prosper" and to become
"valuable". *God is not only a healer. He is someone who teaches
you how to prosper.* He teaches you how to increase your value.
Open yourself up to the God who can teach you how to profit.
God is teaching you how to become rich, how to ascend and how
to prosper. You will receive a revelation from God that will make
you prosperous.

1.   God gave a revelation to Jacob that made him prosper.

And Jacob sent and called Rachel and Leah to the field
unto his flock, and said unto them, I see your father's
countenance, that it is not toward me as before; but the
God of my father hath been with me. And ye know that
with all my power I have served your father. And your
father hath deceived me, and changed my wages ten
times; but God suffered him not to hurt me. If he said
thus, The speckled shall be thy wages; then all the cattle
bare speckled: and if he said thus, The ringstraked shall
be thy hire; then bare all the cattle ringstraked. Thus God
hath taken away the cattle of your father, and given them
to me. AND IT CAME TO PASS AT THE TIME THAT
THE CATTLE CONCEIVED, THAT I LIFTED UP MINE

EYES, AND SAW IN A DREAM, AND, BEHOLD, THE RAMS WHICH LEAPED UPON THE CATTLE WERE RINGSTRAKED, SPECKLED, AND GRISLED. AND THE ANGEL OF GOD SPAKE UNTO ME IN A DREAM, SAYING, JACOB: AND I SAID, HERE AM I. And he said, Lift up now thine eyes, and see, all the rams which leap upon the cattle are ringstraked, speckled, and grisled: for I have seen all that Laban doeth unto thee.

Genesis 31:4-12

This revelation came to Jacob in a dream. Jacob's dream led him to take speckled sheep and it was accepted and made him a millionaire. God gave Jacob a dream in which he saw that the sheep that were flourishing were the spotted ones. Through this dream, Jacob chose to have spotted sheep as his salary. Each time he chose the type of sheep that he would have as his pay, all the sheep would bear that type. Supernaturally, all the wealth of Uncle Laban was directed into the hands of Jacob. Jacob left Laban's house a wealthy man. He had the revelation of this through a dream.

2. God gave supernatural revelation to Job that made him prosper.

ACQUAINT NOW THYSELF WITH HIM, and be at peace: thereby good shall come unto thee. RECEIVE, I PRAY THEE, THE LAW FROM HIS MOUTH, and lay up his words in thine heart. If thou RETURN TO THE ALMIGHTY, THOU SHALT BE BUILT UP, thou shalt put away iniquity far from thy tabernacles. THEN SHALT THOU LAY UP GOLD AS DUST, and the gold of Ophir as the stones of the brooks. Yea, the Almighty shall be thy defence, and THOU SHALT HAVE PLENTY OF SILVER. For then shalt thou have thy delight in the Almighty, and shalt lift up thy face unto God. THOU SHALT MAKE THY PRAYER UNTO HIM, AND HE SHALL HEAR THEE, and thou shalt pay thy vows. Thou shalt also decree a thing, and it shall be established unto thee: and the light shall shine upon thy ways. WHEN MEN ARE CAST DOWN, THEN THOU SHALT SAY, THERE IS LIFTING UP; and he shall save the humble person.

Job 22:21-29

It is amazing that Job, the richest man in the east, was not labouring to be rich. He was labouring to know God. He was labouring to have a revelation of God. The revelation of the word of God is what made Job the richest man in the east. Job had a seven-point plan that led to his amazing wealth. Gold became like dust to him and he had plenty of silver. Knowing God and having a revelation of Him was at the centre of his seven-point plan of prosperity.

Job was labouring to know God and labouring to receive the law of God. Job was coming near to God so that he could be built up. Job was not labouring to be rich. He was labouring to know God. Labour for a revelation of God and all these things will be added unto you.

Job's plan of prosperity was simple. It had seven points:

1. Know God. Acquaint yourself with Him and be at peace.

2. Receive the law of God.

   Receive, I pray thee, the law from his mouth, and lay up his words in your heart.

   Job 22:22

3. Come to God and be built up.

   …return to the Almighty, thou shall be built up…

   Job 22:23

4. Gold, like dust, will be your portion.

   Then thou shalt lay up gold as dust, and the gold of Ophir as the stones of the brooks.

   Job 22:24

5. Silver will be your portion.

> Yea, the Almighty shall be thy defence, and thou shalt have plenty of silver.
>
> Job 22:25

6. God will hear your prayer.

> Thou shalt make thy prayer unto him, and he shall hear thee, and thou shall pay thy vows
>
> Job 22:27

7. When men are down you will be exempted.

> When men are cast down, then thou shalt say, there is a lifting up; and he shall save the humble person.
>
> Job 22:29

3. **God will give you a revelation that will make you shine**. Revelation from God is a light that makes you shine. You will arise and shine because a light has been put on in your life. God gives light to you and this leads to your prosperity. In this beautiful prophecy, we see how the light of God comes into your life leading to your rising and shining. Light is revelation.

ARISE, SHINE; FOR THY LIGHT IS COME, and the glory of the Lord is risen upon thee. For, behold, the darkness shall cover the earth, and gross darkness the people: but the Lord shall arise upon thee, and HIS GLORY SHALL BE SEEN UPON THEE. And the Gentiles shall come to thy light, and kings to the brightness of thy rising. Lift up thine eyes round about, and see: all they gather themselves together, they come to thee: thy sons shall come from far, and thy daughters shall be nursed at thy side. Then thou shalt see, and flow together, and thine heart shall fear, and be enlarged; because the abundance of the sea shall be converted unto thee, the forces of the Gentiles shall come unto thee. The multitude of camels shall cover thee, the dromedaries of Midian and Ephah; all they from Sheba shall come: THEY SHALL BRING GOLD AND INCENSE; and they shall shew forth the praises of the Lord.

Isaiah 60:1-6

CHAPTER 11

Labour to be Associated with Blessed People

And the ark of the Lord continued in the house of Obededom the Gittite three months: and the Lord blessed Obededom, and all his household.

2 Samuel 6:11

Obededom was happy to have the ark present in his house. Everything started working when the Ark of the Covenant came to be in his house. Obededom's family, Obededom's children and Obededom's business all took an upward turn when the Ark of the Covenant came there.

The presence of a blessing can never be discounted. Wisely look for where the blessings can be found and attach yourself firmly to blessed people. Labour to be associated with a blessed person, rather than labouring to be rich!

Instead of labouring to be rich, you must labour to associate with blessed people. Instead of striving for wealth, strive to be associated with blessed people. Why work with all your heart to get money, when you can work with all your heart to be associated with a blessed person? Associate with a blessed person and become blessed!

Association with blessed people is one of the easiest ways to prosper. When a person is super blessed, the blessings often spill over and affect those around him. Just as wealthy people often provide jobs for thousands of others, one blessed person can provide blessings for thousands under his leadership. Sometimes it is far more profitable to be associated with someone who has the obvious blessing of God on his life than to do anything else.

Laban, Jacob's uncle, realised that his nephew had a peculiar blessing on his life. Many people would have been too proud to acknowledge that their young nephew who had come earlier seeking refuge and seeking a job was actually a very blessed person. Most people would have found it difficult to accept that things were going well in their lives because of the presence of a young refugee. Who is there in your life whom God has blessed? A few droplets of the blessing on that person may earn you much more than you could ever do for yourself or get for yourself in thirty years of working hard. Labour not to be rich! Labour to be associated with blessed people! Why not apply yourself to the wisdom of Laban and accept that some people are extra blessed and it is wise to associate with them?

Potiphar, an Egyptian businessman, had his whole family being blessed because of the presence of Joseph. God's eye was on Joseph and God's blessing was on Joseph. Whether as a slave or as a prisoner, he experienced the blessings of God. It is time to recognize this eternal principle.

Countries that hound rich and blessed people are fighting themselves. One blessed person can provide so much for many people.

Those who associated with Paul partook of his grace.

Even as it is meet for me to think this of you all, because I have you in my heart; inasmuch as both in my bonds, and in the defence and confirmation of the gospel, YE ALL ARE PARTAKERS OF MY GRACE.

Philippians 1:7

You must labour for the blessing that comes from associating with blessed people. Associating with blessed people causes you to partake of their grace. It is grace that makes things work out for blessed people. You will receive far more by your association with blessed people than by striving on your own for money. All through the Bible, we see examples of the blessing that comes through association. Three examples stand out:

1. Lot associating with Abraham.

And LOT ALSO, which went with Abram, HAD FLOCKS, and herds, and tents.

Genesis 13:5

Lot had flocks, herds and tents because of his association with Abraham. Abraham is the one who was blessed. We always speak of the blessings of Abraham and not the blessings of Lot. Lot experienced the blessing of fruitfulness because of his association with Abraham. When he separated from Abraham, his whole life was destroyed in the city of Sodom. He became destitute and was "raped" by his daughters. Lot's wife turned into a pillar of salt. Lot turned into a nobody when because of strife, he was separated from Abraham.

2. Laban associating with Jacob.

And Laban said unto him, I pray thee, if I have found favour in thine eyes, tarry: for I HAVE LEARNED BY EXPERIENCE THAT THE LORD HATH BLESSED ME FOR THY SAKE.

Genesis 30:27

Laban also experienced a multiplication of all that he had when Jacob came to live with him. Amazingly, Laban saw through the multiplication of his herds and flocks. Laban saw that God was blessing him because of Jacob. Many people are too proud to see and acknowledge that God is blessing them because of someone.

3. Potiphar associating with Joseph.

And his master saw that the Lord was with him, and that the Lord made all that he did to prosper in his hand. And Joseph found grace in his sight, and he served him: and he made him overseer over his house, and all that he had he put into his hand. And it came to pass from the time that he had made him overseer in his house, and over all that he had, THAT THE LORD BLESSED THE EGYPTIAN'S HOUSE FOR JOSEPH'S SAKE; AND THE BLESSING OF THE LORD WAS UPON ALL THAT HE HAD IN THE HOUSE, AND IN THE FIELD. And he left all that he had in Joseph's hand; and he knew not ought he had, save the bread which he did eat. And Joseph was a goodly person, and well favoured.

Genesis 39:3-6

Potiphar's house was blessed greatly because of Joseph. Joseph's presence in Potiphar's house changed everything. God had no plans of blessing Potiphar. His eye was on Joseph, the seed of Abraham, Isaac and Jacob. Because Potiphar, a wicked unbeliever was associated with Joseph, God decided to bless Potiphar. Many blessings in the world are because of association.

You may earn far more by seeking to be associated with a blessed person than seeking after a higher salary. Most people simply seek for a higher salary. Often, a higher salary does not change things much. It is the blessing of the Lord that really changes lives. Seek to be blessed rather than seeking to be wealthy! Labour to be blessed rather than labouring to be rich!

CHAPTER 12

Labour for Exemption
from Evil

BEHOLD, THE EYE OF THE LORD IS UPON
THEM THAT FEAR HIM, upon them that hope in
his mercy; to deliver their soul from death, AND TO
KEEP THEM ALIVE IN FAMINE. Our soul waiteth
for the Lord: he is our help and our shield.

Psalms 33:18-20

The eye of the Lord is upon you. Because you fear God, your soul will be exempted from the evil that is lurking around.

God can keep you alive in a famine. When everyone else is destroyed by the poverty and financial difficulty, you will survive.

Instead of labouring to be rich, you must labour for the blessing of being exempted from evil. Instead of striving for wealth, strive to be exempted from the curses that are multiplying over the planet. Why work with all your heart to get rich, when you can work with all your heart for the blessing of "exemption". Strive to be exempted from the many evils that are in the world.

There are many evils sweeping through the earth today. Just look around you and you will see poverty, disease, tragedy, war and famine. Put on the news and you may even be frightened about what is happening now. What is going to be the next big tragedy? Tragedies can wipe out all your life's achievements. Tragedies can make nonsense of your family, your money and even of your house. What is the use of your big house if there is no one to live in it? What is the use of your riches if you are not well enough to enjoy them?

All through the Bible, we see examples of how God exempted His people from the curses and tragedies that were raging around. Would you not want God to exempt you from the wickedness in the world? Instead of labouring to be rich, labour to be exempted from the curse that is lurking around by day and by night.

All through the Bible, God exempts His people from the judgments that are coming.

In the great flood, He exempted Noah from destruction!

In the destruction of Sodom and Gomorrah He exempted Lot and his family from the fire! You will be exempted from the judgment of the wicked! All those who had laboured to be rich in Sodom and Gomorrah were shocked as their houses were burnt to the ground.

Arise and shine, your light has come! Gross darkness will cover the earth but you will be exempted from the world's darkness. The glory of the Lord will be seen upon you.

There is no need to seek a better place to live. Gross darkness is going to cover the whole world. You need the power of God to exempt you from the darkness in the world. It is actually in the gross darkness that the glory of the Lord will arise on you.

People choose to go to nations because they feel that they will be rich and prosperous there. They are attracted by bright colours and flashing lights! But flashing lights and bright colours never made any one prosperous! Labour to be exempted from the evil rather than labouring to be rich. Labour to be one of the few that God exempts.

In the Psalms, God promises that He will keep you alive in the time of famine. A famine is the same as an economic crisis. Africa is in a perpetual economic depression. But that is where the glory of the Lord can arise. Indeed, the seed of the righteous shall be delivered. A thousand shall fall on your side and ten thousand on your right hand, but God will exempt you. Labour to escape the evils of this world rather than following the wealthy flashing lights of rich cities.

Why God Will Exempt You

1. God will exempt you from evil because He knows how to extract the godly from temptations.

And spared not the old world, but saved Noah the eighth person, a preacher of righteousness, bringing in the flood upon the world of the ungodly; And turning the cities of Sodom and Gomorrha into ashes condemned them with an overthrow, making them an ensample unto those that after should live ungodly; And delivered just Lot, vexed with the filthy conversation of the wicked: (For that righteous man dwelling among them, in seeing and hearing, vexed his

81

righteous soul from day to day with their unlawful deeds;)
THE LORD KNOWETH HOW TO DELIVER THE
GODLY OUT OF TEMPTATIONS, AND TO RESERVE
THE UNJUST UNTO THE DAY OF JUDGMENT TO
BE PUNISHED:

2 Peter 2:5-9

Most armies know how to extract their soldiers from dangerous places where they are trapped. They will send troops to get them out. They will send commandos to extract them miraculously from their captors. They will spend money to buy their release from hijackers and kidnappers. They will risk lives to save their lives. There are many films that are dedicated to the saving of a few captured soldiers. Everyone loves to watch how dedicated and sacrificial soldiers are saved from their captors.

If secular and wicked unbelievers know how to extract their own from the field, do you think God cannot extract you from this world? God can extract you from this dark world and save you from the evil that is sweeping through. God can stretch out His long arm and rescue you from any situation. God's arm is very long indeed! He will deliver you! He will save you! He will exempt you! You will be blessed with the blessing of exemption.

2. God will exempt you from evil because He will not put bitter as sweet and sweet as bitter.

Woe unto them that call evil good, and good evil; that put darkness for light, and light for darkness; that put bitter for sweet, and sweet for bitter!

Isaiah 5:20

In other words, God will not treat the sweet as He treats the bitter. How do you treat sweet things? You suck sweet things endlessly. How do you treat bitter things? You spit them out of your mouth. God will not treat His sweet children the same way as He treats His bitter children. The sweet ones will be exempted from being spat out.

3. God will exempt you from the darkness coming on the whole earth because of His glory.

Arise, shine; for thy light is come, and the glory of the Lord is risen upon thee. For, behold, the darkness shall cover the earth, AND GROSS DARKNESS THE PEOPLE: BUT THE LORD SHALL ARISE UPON THEE, and HIS GLORY SHALL BE SEEN upon thee.

Isaiah 60:1-2

This famous scripture describes the exemption that comes on God's people. In the midst of gross darkness, a light starts to shine. Darkness covers the whole earth. Everyone seems to be plunged into deep darkness. What is this darkness? This darkness is the darkness of poverty, the darkness of sickness, the darkness of sin, the darkness of defeat, the darkness of frustration, the darkness of humiliation, the darkness of failure and the darkness of death. In the midst of this overwhelming darkness, you will begin to be a beacon of salvation, light and hope. When everyone is dying, you will have the blessing of exemption. When everyone is diagnosed with an evil disease, you will be spared. When everyone is defeated, you will be successful. You will rise and shine in the midst of darkness because God has given you the blessing of being exempted from the effect of gross darkness.

4. God will exempt you from evil times of financial difficulties and economic crises because you are upright.

THE LORD KNOWETH THE DAYS OF THE UPRIGHT: AND THEIR INHERITANCE SHALL BE FOR EVER. THEY SHALL NOT BE ASHAMED IN THE EVIL TIME: AND IN THE DAYS OF FAMINE THEY SHALL BE SATISFIED. But the wicked shall perish, and the enemies of the Lord shall be as the fat of lambs: they shall consume; into smoke shall they consume away. The wicked borroweth, and payeth not again: but the righteous

83

sheweth mercy, and giveth. For such as be blessed of him shall inherit the earth; and they that be cursed of him shall be cut off.

Psalms 37:18-22

The world is hurtling towards financial disaster. Most of the world's financial systems are based on deception. Nations are up to their necks in debts! Banks are up to their necks in debt! Much of the impressive prosperity that we see bandied around is actually fake prosperity. There is going to be more confusion! There is going to be more debt! There is going to be more difficulty!

Many African nations are failed states. Their governments have simply been unable to rule properly since independence. Many governments are make-believe regimes that are not really in control. Many nations could be overwhelmed and completely taken over by stronger nations if they so desired. It would not take one week to completely take over many African states. The weakness of their currencies, the weakness of their leadership and their incompetence are easy to see. Such governments only create more and more poverty for their people. Some governments are actually happy to have famines because they feel it reduces their population to manageable levels.

Dear friend, expect more famines and more confusion in the world. Instead of labouring to be rich in this messed up world, labour for the blessing of being exempted from the famine that is sweeping through large parts of the world.

5. **God will exempt you from the punishment coming to the wicked because of your righteousness.**

They that are of a froward heart are abomination to the Lord: but such as are upright in their way are his delight. Though hand join in hand, THE WICKED SHALL NOT BE UNPUNISHED: BUT THE SEED OF THE RIGHTEOUS SHALL BE DELIVERED.

Proverbs 11:20-21

You cannot be made righteous except through the blood of Jesus. You are therefore exempted from eternal damnation and punishment because of the blood of Jesus.

What shall it profit a man if he gains the whole world but is not exempted from eternal damnation? What will your properties in New York do for you when you are in hell? Labour to be exempted from the eternal damnation that is coming upon the whole world. Labour for the blessing of being exempted from the lake of fire!

Indeed, you will be exempted from the punishment that is coming to the world. Human beings have built state-of-the-art prisons to keep criminals and sinners out of society. God has also built a state-of-the-art prison for the unrepentant sinners and criminals of this world. I am happy to announce to you that you will be exempted from going to this prison because of the blood of Jesus! Labour to be exempted from the torment and the punishment that will be released on those who do not believe.

6. God will exempt you from evil because you make the Lord your habitation.

A thousand shall fall at thy side, and ten thousand at thy right hand; but it shall not come nigh thee. Only with thine eyes shalt thou behold and see the reward of the wicked. BECAUSE THOU HAST MADE THE LORD, WHICH IS MY REFUGE, EVEN THE MOST HIGH, THY HABITATION; there shall no evil befall thee, neither shall any plague come nigh thy dwelling.

Psalms 91:7-10

Perhaps, this scripture best describes the blessing of exemption! A thousand will fall at your side and ten thousand at your right hand. But nothing happens to you! That is the blessing of exemption! Receive it right now! Be delivered from the evil that happens to thousands of people around you!

7.   God will exempt you from evil because you serve Him.

And they shall be mine, saith the Lord of hosts, in that day
when I make up my jewels; and I WILL SPARE THEM,
AS A MAN SPARETH HIS OWN SON THAT SERVETH
HIM.   Then shall ye return, and discern between the
righteous and the wicked, between him that serveth God
and him that serveth him not.

Malachi 3:17-18

God will spare you because you serve Him. To be spared is
to be exempted from evil. That is a great blessing! Do you want
God to save you and spare you? How relieved we are when we
are spared evil! You realise that it could have happened to you.
You realise that you could have been the one to perish. God had
mercy on you and spared your life. The blessing of exemption
cannot be bought with money. It is a great blessing for God to
excuse you from the commotion, confusion and judgment that is
destined for this world.

CHAPTER 13

Labour for the Blessing of the Holy Spirit

The Holy Spirit will give you the greatest help you will ever receive. The Holy Spirit is the Helper. He helps in financial situations as well.

Instead of labouring to be rich, you must labour to receive the Holy Spirit. Instead of striving for wealth, strive for the Holy Spirit. Why work with all your heart to get money, when you can work with all your heart to receive the Holy Spirit? The Holy Spirit is what you need. You need the Holy Spirit far more than you need riches.

Through the Holy Spirit, you will have wisdom, understanding and counsel. The Spirit of wisdom will bring you into great wealth. The Holy Spirit is the One who will lead you into green pastures where you will never lack.

The mighty Holy Spirit is the One who brings the help that you need. Remember that the Holy Spirit is your helper. He will help you in every area of your life. You will be helped in your financial situation when you tap into the great help that comes from the Holy Spirit. This is how the Holy Spirit will help you.

1. Labour for the Holy Spirit because He will make you into a supernatural being.

For as many as are led by the Spirit of God, they are the sons of God.

Romans 8:14

Labour not to be rich! Labour for the Holy Spirit! When you have the Holy Spirit, He will lead you. When He leads you, you will be like a son of God. Sons of God are like angels. Sons of God are supernatural beings. In the book of Job we see the sons of God presenting themselves to the Lord.

Now there was a day when the sons of God came to present themselves before the Lord, and Satan came also among them.

Job 1:6

When you become one of the sons of God, you become supernatural in everything you do. You are successful when others are not. You live when others die. You flourish when others are poor. That is what it means to be a son of God. Indeed, the Holy Spirit is the greatest gift given to human beings. It is the Holy Spirit who lifts us out of our frail, human, failure-ridden state. The Holy Spirit makes us rise above the weak and dishonourable flesh. This is how a sinful man can be a prophet or a servant of God. Only the presence of the Holy Spirit can change everything about us.

Supernatural wealth will come to the supernatural sons of God through the power of the Holy Spirit. When you are a son of God, you will be led by the Spirit to the hidden riches of secret places. Through the power of God, you will experience all the wealth you cannot get for yourself by labouring to be rich.

2. Labour for the Spirit to be poured out from on high because you will become fruitful.

Upon the land of my people shall come up thorns and briers; yea, upon all the houses of joy in the joyous city: Because the palaces shall be forsaken; the multitude of the city shall be left; the forts and towers shall be for dens for ever, a joy of wild asses, a pasture of flocks; UNTIL THE SPIRIT BE POURED UPON US FROM ON HIGH, AND THE WILDERNESS BE A FRUITFUL FIELD, AND THE FRUITFUL FIELD BE COUNTED FOR A FOREST.

Isaiah 32:13-15

When the Holy Spirit is poured out from on high, there is a release of fruitfulness. Fruitfulness is what you need to prosper. When you are fruitful, your business will flourish and all your work will increase. You can see that there is a direct correlation between becoming fruitful and the Holy Spirit being poured out on you.

Labour for the windows of heaven to be opened so that the Holy Spirit is poured out on you. The windows of heaven are spiritual windows that will release spiritual blessings upon you. One of the wonderful blessings that can be poured upon you is the Holy Spirit.

3. Labour for the Holy Spirit's divine direction for your life.

The Lord is my shepherd; I shall not want. He maketh me to lie down in green pastures: he leadeth me beside the still waters.

Psalms 23:1-2

The Holy Spirit gives divine guidance that leads to prosperity through the voice of the Shepherd. The Lord is your Shepherd. You will never be in need. Trust the Holy Spirit. His direction is the master key to becoming a supernatural person who receives supernatural provision. The Holy Spirit will lead you straight to the hidden riches of secret places.

4. Labour for the Holy Spirit who alone can give waters in the desert.

And THEY THIRSTED NOT WHEN HE LED THEM THROUGH THE DESERTS: he caused the waters to flow out of the rock for them: he clave the rock also, and THE WATERS GUSHED OUT.

Isaiah 48:21

When the Holy Spirit comes on your life, He will lead you through deserts and you will not die there. Instead of dying in the desert you will flourish and prosper there. Waters will be gushing out in the very place where everyone thought you would die of thirst. The Holy Spirit is your master key to surviving financial deserts.

CHAPTER 14

Labour for the Blessing of Favour

Instead of labouring to be rich, you must labour for the blessing of being favoured. Instead of striving for wealth, strive to be favoured and chosen. Why work with all your heart to get money, when you can work with all your heart to have favour. When you are favoured, you will not have to work for many things that others are dying for. A favoured person is a blessed person! A favoured person receives many supernatural gifts!

Favour is important. Favour is all about being chosen without any specific reason given. To have favour is to be chosen! From a certain point onwards, promotion does not come through your examinations or class tests. Life is all about favour and being chosen. The biggest promotions and the biggest positions are never based on education or qualifications. They are based on favour.

One of the most important experiences for a woman is to be chosen by a man for marriage. Unfortunately, there is no examination for this. When a man chooses a woman, he can hardly explain why he chose her. There are often many people just like the girl he chose. And yet he chooses her!

That is favour! When Esther was eventually chosen, there was no good reason given. The biggest opportunities are often given by unexplained decisions.

The Bible is full of teachings and revelations on the subject of favour. This is because so many things come through favour. Therefore, labour for favour rather than labouring to be rich. Understand the principles that work behind favour. Do everything you can to be favoured. Instead of aiming to be rich, aim to be a "favoured favourite."

All through the Scripture, the Holy Spirit gave divine favour to people and that led to their prosperity.

Labour to Have Favour because Favour Leads to Wealth

1. **The Israelites had favour and they walked away with the wealth of Egypt.**

The Egyptians laboured for riches. The Israelites received favour. The Egyptians who had laboured for riches handed them over to the Israelites who were favoured. When God favours you, people will hand over their riches to you. People who have laboured all their lives for riches will give it to you whom God has favoured.

> And I WILL GIVE THIS PEOPLE FAVOUR in the sight of the Egyptians: and it shall come to pass, that, when ye go, YE SHALL NOT GO EMPTY:
>
> Exodus 3:21

> And the children of Israel did according to the word of Moses; and they borrowed of the Egyptians jewels of silver, and jewels of gold, and raiment: AND THE LORD GAVE THE PEOPLE FAVOUR IN THE SIGHT OF THE

EGYPTIANS, SO THAT THEY LENT UNTO THEM SUCH THINGS AS THEY REQUIRED. And they spoiled the Egyptians.

Exodus 12:35-36

2. Ruth found favour with Boaz and received a job and a husband.

You will never lack a husband nor a job from now onwards! Favour is given to you and people will choose you! Why labour for riches when you can labour to be favoured?

THEN SHE FELL ON HER FACE, AND BOWED HERSELF TO THE GROUND, AND SAID UNTO HIM, WHY HAVE I FOUND GRACE IN THINE EYES, THAT THOU SHOULDEST TAKE KNOWLEDGE OF ME, SEEING I AM A STRANGER? And Boaz answered and said unto her, It hath fully been shewed me, all that thou hast done unto thy mother in law since the death of thine husband: and how thou hast left thy father and thy mother, and the land of thy nativity, and art come unto a people which thou knewest not heretofore. The Lord recompense thy work, and a full reward be given thee of the Lord God of Israel, under whose wings thou art come to trust. THEN SHE SAID, LET ME FIND FAVOUR IN THY SIGHT, MY LORD; FOR THAT THOU HAST COMFORTED ME, and for that thou hast spoken friendly unto thine handmaid, though I be not like unto one of thine handmaidens. And Boaz said unto her, At mealtime come thou hither, and eat of the bread, and dip thy morsel in the vinegar. And she sat beside the reapers: and he reached her parched corn, and she did eat, and was sufficed, and left.

Ruth 2:10-14

3. Joseph found favour in Egypt and this made him a national hero and a governor.

You will receive high-up positions as God favours you. Why labour for riches when you can labour to be favoured?

And the patriarchs, moved with envy, SOLD JOSEPH INTO EGYPT: BUT GOD WAS WITH HIM, AND DELIVERED HIM OUT OF ALL HIS AFFLICTIONS, AND GAVE HIM FAVOUR and wisdom in the sight of Pharaoh king of Egypt; and he made him governor over Egypt and all his house.

Acts 7:9-10

4. Daniel was favoured and received exemptions and privileges in his job.

But Daniel purposed in his heart that he would not defile himself with the portion of the king's meat, nor with the wine which he drank: therefore he requested of the prince of the eunuchs that he might not defile himself. NOW GOD HAD BROUGHT DANIEL INTO FAVOUR AND TENDER LOVE WITH THE PRINCE OF THE EUNUCHS.

Daniel 1:8-9

You will receive exemptions and privileges in the day that you have favour. Labour to receive favour rather than labouring to be rich. Daniel and his friends did not need riches. They needed favour. Riches would not have set them free. Favour gave them a better life and a better job. Why should you labour for riches when you can labour for the favour of God?

5. David was favoured and he got a job in the king's palace.

And Jesse took an ass laden with bread, and a bottle of wine, and a kid, and sent them by David his son unto Saul. And David came to Saul, and stood before him: and he loved him greatly; and he became his armourbearer. And Saul sent to Jesse, saying, LET DAVID, I PRAY THEE, STAND BEFORE ME; FOR HE HATH FOUND FAVOUR IN MY SIGHT.

1 Samuel 16:20-22

Favour is what causes you to become a national hero or a darling boy. Labour for favour! Don't waste your time labouring to be rich. Labour to be favoured! I do not know what David did in the king's court. The king just loved him and chose him to be his personal assistant. You will soon be chosen to be a personal assistant. You will soon be chosen to be a national hero! You will soon be chosen to be a darling boy! You will soon be chosen to be a favoured daughter! Labour to be chosen rather than labouring to be rich!

6. Mary was favoured and became the mother of Jesus.

And in the sixth month the angel Gabriel was sent from God unto a city of Galilee, named Nazareth, To a virgin espoused to a man whose name was Joseph, of the house of David; and the virgin's name was Mary. And the angel came in unto her, and said, HAIL, THOU THAT ART HIGHLY FAVOURED, THE LORD IS WITH THEE: BLESSED ART THOU AMONG WOMEN. And when she saw him, she was troubled at his saying, and cast in her mind what manner of salutation this should be.

Luke 1:26-29

When Mary received favour, she became the mother of God and perhaps the most honoured woman of all time. The favour upon a person that is chosen out of the whole world is a wonder and a blessing. This great choosing and selection comes only from the power of God. The favour of God is a unique blessing that falls on those whom God chooses.

CHAPTER 15

How to Labour for the Blessing of Favour

1. Labour for favour by looking young and acting young.

The Lord shall bring a nation against thee from far, from the end of the earth, as swift as the eagle flieth; a nation whose tongue thou shalt not understand; A nation of fierce countenance, WHICH SHALL NOT REGARD THE PERSON OF THE OLD, NOR SHEW FAVOUR TO THE YOUNG:

Deuteronomy 28:49-50

Let there be none to extend mercy unto him: NEITHER LET THERE BE ANY TO FAVOUR HIS FATHERLESS CHILDREN.

Psalms 109:12

Children are often given special treatment. Many young people want to look older. They do not realise that youthfulness is favoured. The older you look, the less you are chosen for things.

Most people would favour children over adults. I once told a professional footballer to cut his hair and look as young as he really was. I told him, "Your coach will choose you because you look like a boy and not a man."

Make yourself a child and you are likely to be chosen. If you paint yourself like an experienced woman who has run through the city, you are not likely to receive favour from certain quarters.

2. Labour for favour by being merciful and truthful.

LET NOT MERCY AND TRUTH FORSAKE THEE: bind them about thy neck; write them upon the table of thine heart: SO SHALT THOU FIND FAVOUR and good understanding in the sight of God and man.

Proverbs 3:3-4

Telling the truth and being merciful are very important when it comes to finding favour. It is very distasteful to see a supervisor being nasty to the few people under his power, when you know that he himself has so many shortcomings. When a supervisor is merciful to others you are more attracted to him.

3. Labour for favour by being righteous.

FOR THOU, LORD, WILT BLESS THE RIGHTEOUS; WITH FAVOUR wilt thou compass him as with a shield.

Psalms 5:12

Righteousness is attractive. When people lose their holiness and purity, they lose favour. Sin causes you to lose favour. Put away your sin and unrighteous life. God will favour you and choose you!

4. Labour for favour by having a good understanding of issues.

Favour is always given to people who understand the leader. You may be a little child but if the king realises that you understand his issues, you will have his favour. Arguments make you lose favour. Arguments reveal your stubborn mind. Arguments reveal that you are a blockhead and that you cannot understand simple things when they are pointed out to you.

GOOD UNDERSTANDING GIVETH FAVOUR: but the way of transgressors is hard.

Proverbs 13:15

5. Labour for favour in the season for favour.

Thou shalt arise, and have mercy upon Zion: FOR THE TIME TO FAVOUR HER, YEA, THE SET TIME, IS COME.

Psalms 102:13

There is a season for favour. There is a time when you must be chosen. Favour does not come all the time. There is a time and a season when God decides to favour you. In your season, you will be chosen and recognized. There is a season in which a woman is chosen for marriage. After that season it is unlikely that she will ever be chosen.

6. Labour for the Holy Spirit who gives favour.

Then they that gladly received his word were baptized: and the same day there were added unto them about three thousand souls. And they continued stedfastly in the apostles' doctrine and fellowship, and in breaking of bread, and in prayers. And fear came upon every soul: and many wonders and signs were done by the apostles. AND ALL THAT BELIEVED WERE TOGETHER, AND HAD ALL THINGS COMMON; ... PRAISING GOD, AND HAVING FAVOUR WITH ALL THE PEOPLE. And the Lord added to the church daily such as should be saved.

Acts 2:41-44, 47

The Holy Spirit was poured out on the early church and that produced favour. The church received much favour from the people. This meant that many people chose the early church as their church. Many people join a church when favour is upon it. Many people will come to your shop when there is favour upon your business.

7.   Labour for favour by praying for it.

Pray for favour because it is God who gives favour. Favour is something you can seek for. Favour is something you can pray for.

HE SHALL PRAY UNTO GOD, AND HE WILL BE FAVOURABLE UNTO HIM: and he shall see his face with joy: for he will render unto man his righteousness.

Job 33:26